The Royal Path

Practical Lessons on Yoga

The Royal Path

Practical Lessons on Yoga

Swami Rama

HIMALAYAN INSTITUTE®

PRESS

HONESDALE, PENNSYLVANIA, USA

The Himalayan Institute Press
952 Bethany Turnpike
Honesdale, PA 18431 USA

Originally published as *Lectures on Yoga*
© 1979 by Swami Rama
© 1996, 1998 by The Himalayan International Institute of
Yoga Science and Philosophy of the USA
All rights reserved. Printed in China

9 8 7 6 5 4 3 2 1

Cover design by Robert Aulicino

The paper used in this publication meets the minimum require-
ments of the American National Standard for Information
Sciences—Permanence of Paper for Printed Library Materials,
ANSI Z39.48-1984.

ISBN-13: 978-0-8938-9152-7
ISBN-10: 0-89389-152-5

Contents

Preface

THERE ARE SEVEN ancient schools of Indian philosophy, ranging from a materialistic point of view similar in many respects to the current Western perspective, to its diametric opposite in which matter is considered a mere shadow of spirit. The Sankhya and Yoga schools take a point midway between these two extremes. Yoga deals with the experiential aspects of man's liberation from imperfection and suffering and offers practical methods for attaining this state. It uses the philosophical doctrines of Sankhya as its basis.

Sankhya, which was founded by the sage Kapila around 600 B.C., admits of two ultimate realities: *purusha,* or cosmic consciousness, and *prakriti,* or elemental matter. The universe evolves out of matter, but is permeated by consciousness. Yoga is based on this scheme of evolution in man—the microcosm—but focuses on the practical aspects of involution, or the return of consciousness from identification with a material body and mind to ultimate consciousness.

The main teaching of yoga is that man's innermost nature is divine but that he is unaware of this and mistakes himself for his body and intellect—both of which exist within the realm of matter and therefore are subject to decay and death. All of man's misery is a consequence of this false identification. Yoga leads one to the direct experience of his inner Self, his true identity. With such realization comes liberation from all human imperfections.

There are many paths to realization of the Self, just as the many spokes from the rim of a wheel meet at the hub. The word *yoga* is used in a generic sense for all these different paths. Some of them are: karma yoga, the path of action; bhakti yoga, the path of devotion; jnana yoga, the path of knowledge; kundalini yoga, the path of awakening latent spiritual power; and raja yoga, the royal path.

Raja yoga, which is the subject of this book, encompasses the teachings of all these different paths. It concerns itself with three dimensions—the physical, the mental, and the spiritual. Through the methods of raja yoga one achieves mastery of all three realms and is led to full realization of the Self.

The teachings of raja yoga go back many thousands of years. Little is known of their beginnings, but they are considered to be revealed teachings of divine origin. Somewhere around 200 B.C., they were systematized by the sage Patanjali, who organized the teachings into 196 *sutras,* or aphorisms, called the *Yoga Sutra.* This text consists of four *padas,* or chapters. The first deals with *samadhi,* the state of self-realization, the second with the practical means by which this can be achieved, the third with the powers that manifest themselves in one who treads the path of yoga, while the last chapter deals with *kaivalya,* or liberation.

Raja yoga, also known as *ashtanga* yoga or the eightfold path, outlines the practical means of achieving the state of self-realization. It is made up of eight *angas,* or limbs: *yama, niyama, asana, pranayama, pratyahara, dharana, dhyana,* and *samadhi.* The first five are called the external limbs, the last three are internal. The yamas and niyamas constitute the moral code of yoga and help one cultivate the right mental attitude. Asana, or posture, aims at physical well-being and control over the body, for a healthy body is a prerequisite for a healthy and controlled mind. Pranayama is control of prana, or life force, achieved through control of the most gross manifestation of *prana*—the breath. One can regulate the mind only if one can regulate one's breathing. Pratyahara is withdrawal of the senses and is necessary if one is to achieve tranquility of mind.

The internal limbs focus more directly on control of the mind. Dharana is attention and concentration; it helps to bring the diffuse mind to a point of focus. Prolonged dharana leads to a state of dhyana, or meditation, characterized by one-pointedness of the mind, while prolonged dhyana leads to samadhi, the state of self-realization. Here the mind is transcended, and one becomes aware of the Self and is ultimately united with it. This state is characterized by *sat-chit-ananda*, or existence, consciousness, and bliss. By expanding his consciousness, the practitioner becomes one with the ultimate reality.

Raja yoga is, therefore, a systematic and scientific discipline that leads one to ultimate truth. Most religions teach a person what to do; raja yoga teaches one how to be. Unlike religion, it does not impose unquestioning faith but encourages healthy discrimination. It leads finally to liberation.

By following the path prescribed, we can verify for ourselves its central hypothesis—that our true nature is divine. Raja yoga is therefore not only an ancient, esoteric Eastern philosophy, but also a practical, systematic, and scientific quest for the infinite, as relevant and necessary in the modern West as it was in ancient India. If incorporated into modern education, raja yoga would equip our children to deal with the conflicts, frustrations, and turmoil inevitable in all modern societies. Through it, we can realize our fullest potential for creative thought and action. Furthermore, through raja yoga we can transcend all human limitations and experience our true nature.

· CHAPTER ONE ·

What Is Yoga?

THE WORD *YOGA* is much overused and misunderstood these days, for our present age is one of faddism, and yoga is often reduced to the status of a fad. Many false and incomplete teachings have been propagated in its name. It has been subject to commercial exploitation, and one small aspect of yoga—the physical postures—is often taken to be the whole of yoga. Many people in the West think it is a health and beauty cult, while others think it is a religion. All of this has obscured the real meaning of yoga. Let me try to give you a glimpse of its true nature.

Yoga is a systematic science; its teachings are an integral part of most religions, but yoga itself is not a religion. Most religions teach what to do, but yoga teaches how to be. Yet yoga practices, described in symbolic language, may be found in the sacred scriptures of most religions. The book of Genesis and the book of Revelation contain such teachings, and in the book of Psalms there are many references to methods of meditation, for example Psalms 119:15, 23, 49, and 77. There is also considerable similarity between Sankhya, the underlying philosophy upon which yoga is based, and the teachings found in Judaism. Aspects of the yogic science of breath, for instance, can be found in the Kabbalah, where the link between breath and spirit has always been acknowledged.

In the Christian tradition, Saint Francis of Assisi was one of the greatest yogis that the West has produced. Saint Bernard, Saint Ignatius, Saint Teresa, Saint John of the Cross, Dionysius, and Meister Eckhart were also great Christian yogis. Mystics of all religions have practiced yoga in one form or another. However, with the passage of time, the symbolic language in which these teachings were veiled has been misinterpreted, so that much of the original teaching has been lost or distorted. But these same teachings are alive within the tradition of yoga even today. Yoga is not an esoteric Eastern philosophy; it is a practical, systematic, and scientific quest for perfection, as relevant today as it was in ancient times, as relevant in the West as it is in the East.

The origins of yoga are obscure; they go back many thousands of years and are considered to be divine rather than human. India is a stronghold of this science because the original purity of the teachings has been maintained there. Yoga teachings have been handed down through a living tradition, the tradition of master and disciple. Yoga teachings were systematized by a sage named Patanjali, who codified the teachings into 196 *sutras,* or short aphorisms, around 200 B.C. There are several manuals and manuscripts, not yet translated into English or any other modern language, which help in understanding and practicing the aphorisms of Patanjali, but there are also well-known commentaries on the sutras, such as those of Vyasa and Vachaspati-Misra.

The central teaching of yoga is that man's true nature is divine, perfect, and infinite. He is unaware of this divinity because he falsely identifies himself with his body, mind, and the objects of the external world. This false identification, in turn, makes him think he is imperfect and limited, subject to sorrow, decay, and death because his mind and body are subject to the limitations of time, space, and causation. Through the meditative methods of yoga, however, man can cast off this ignorance and become aware of his own true self, which is pure and free from all imperfections. The Sanskrit word *yoga* comes from the root *yuj*, meaning "to join together, or unite." Yoga represents the union of the individual self, or *Atman,* with the supreme universal Self, or *Paramatman.* This is the union of man with absolute reality. The same concept is described in the Bible by the word *yoke,* meaning "mystic union."

The modern age is a machine age. Most modern societies are obsessed by power, and much time and effort are wasted in trying to discover more powerful and more destructive weapons. Technology has made rapid progress, but man has not. He has learned to harness atomic energy, but is unable to control his own senses and his own mind. The danger of atomic weapons lies not in the powerful destructive devices themselves; it arises because of the uncontrolled minds of the men who are corrupted by their power.

All of man's efforts have been directed outward, and little evolution has taken place in his inner world. His instincts, urges, passions, emotions, thoughts, and actions are as primitive today as they were in less advanced ages. He is engrossed in ignorance which is characterized by restlessness, a blind clinging to earthly existence, perverted individualism, voluptuous abandonment to sensual pleasures, violence, strife, and discord.

In his ignorance, man chases the fleeting shadows of wealth, position, and power, but he can derive no real happiness from finite objects that are conditioned by time, space, and causation. His wants are insatiable, and he is always dissatisfied. One dollar of pleasure is mixed with ninety-nine dollars of pain, fear, and worry. True happiness, inner peace, and contentment elude him. In affluent societies there are many men who have satisfied their basic needs, who have many comforts and luxuries as well as sizable savings, men who have achieved prestige and a position of power in their professions, who have healthy and intelligent families—yet they are discontent. In spite of everything they have, there is still something lacking in their lives, and they continue to search for it in the outside world.

Little do they realize that what they lack is inner peace, which the world outside can never give them. Few truly realize that happiness is a state of mind, that amidst the din and boisterous bustle of worldly activities there are moments of tranquility and peace when the mind soars above temporary pleasures and reflects on the higher mysteries of life. In these moments every man is a philosopher. He then begins to search for the truth, and discrimination dawns on him. If such a man adopts the meditative life, even amidst his worldly activities, he will eventually attain the highest wisdom and the highest bliss of self-realization.

The whole process of yoga is an ascent into the purity of that absolute perfection, which is the original state of man. It implies, therefore, the removal of enveloping impurities, the stilling of lower feelings and thoughts, and the establishment of a state of perfect balance and harmony. All the methods of yoga have ethical and moral perfection as their basis, and thus a new world order of love could easily be effected by the adoption of even the simplest and most fundamental observances of yogic discipline.

The greatest problem for the beginner is his inherent restlessness of mind. Mind, by its very nature, is ever outgoing and unsteady. The highest state of meditation, however, requires a one-pointed mind, free from attachments and worldly desires. This is why attachment of the mind toward worldly objects is the archenemy of the student of yoga. To reach subtler levels of consciousness one needs willpower, discrimination, and firm control of the mind, as well as the ability to consciously direct its powers toward the desired end. This is possible only through a resolute turning away from worldly attachments, a determined effacement of the ego, a deliberate stoppage of all inharmonious mental processes, and a constant dwelling on the ultimate goal.

To achieve this a person need not renounce home and society and retire to the solitude of a mountain cave. Anyone can achieve a state of nonattachment and desirelessness at home, while engaging in worldly activities, if yogic discipline becomes a part of daily life. True renunciation of worldly desires is a mental state; it does not necessarily need to be a physical act of renunciation. But success is possible only with constant and intense practice, always keeping in mind that the ultimate aim is perfection and bliss.

Without nonattachment, no spiritual progress is possible. There are four stages of nonattachment. The first is to make a sincere attempt not to allow the mind to dwell on sensual objects. When objects beckon the student he should endeavor to free himself from those attractions. With the gradual dawning of discrimination, nonattachment develops and equilibrium is established. This is the second stage. When the senses have been subdued (the third stage), the mind responds with hatred and affection for worldly objects because it can function independently of the senses. In the higher stages of nonattachment the objects of the world do not tempt one at all. The senses are under control, and the mind is perfectly free from likes and dislikes and all other pairs of opposites. This is the fourth stage. The aspirant has now gained independence and supremacy.

Let us now consider the prerequisites for treading the path of yoga toward spiritual enlightenment. Good health, a sound mind, sincerity, and a burning desire for liberation from human imperfections are necessary requirements. Good health is ensured by a simple and well-regulated diet, adequate sleep, some physical exercise, and relaxation. Purity of food leads to purity of mind. Heavy food leads to inertia. Milk, fruits, fresh vegetables, nuts, and the like are helpful if they are in proper balance.

One also needs a suitable place to practice yoga exercises and to meditate. It should be maintained at a moderate temperature throughout the year and should be well-ventilated, clean, quiet, and free from dampness. In addition, since all distractions, disturbances, and diseases arise from an imbalance of the three *doshas*—wind, bile, and phlegm (too much phlegm, for instance, makes the body heavy, inert, and stiff), one should choose one's diet and the place for practice so as to maintain a balance of these three.

Yoga science has two aspects—theoretical and practical. Theory can be learned through books and scriptures but a perfect guide, or guru, is needed for the practical aspect. The word *guru* means "one who dispels the darkness of ignorance," and he is needed because in yoga there are several different methods that work toward the same goal of perfection. Only a guru can select and prescribe one that is suitable to the upbringing, circumstances, mind, and nature of the student. A person who tries to learn the practical aspect of yoga through books or from attending a few lectures is often bewildered by the great variety and diversity of techniques. He gains nothing by trying a little of everything, and even if he is sincere, his effort is wasted. A true yogi will always lead the student systematically through the complex stages of yoga to the ultimate state of perfection.

These days there are many yogis who claim to be perfect masters, and it is hard to know how to distinguish the true guru from the many imposters. But when a student prepares himself by increasing his mental capacities, he starts discriminating between right and wrong and between useful and useless values and becomes able to evaluate various teachers accordingly. The Upanishads, ancient yogic scriptures, state that when the disciple is ready, the master appears. This means that when a student has an intense desire for truth in his heart he will receive divine help sooner or later. Fortunate indeed is a student who has the blessings and guidance of a guru.

As mentioned earlier, there are many different methods of yoga, all leading to the same goal of self-realization. The methods vary so as to accommodate varying temperaments and capacities, but they are like different spokes of a wheel, they all meet at the same center—self-realization. The different paths of yoga are not mutually exclusive; they merely represent a difference of emphasis. Let us briefly consider some of these different paths.

Karma yoga, the yoga of action. This path teaches one to do one's own duty skillfully and selflessly, dedicating the fruits of his actions to humanity. This yoga helps one to live successfully in the world while remaining above it, unaffected by worldly fetters.

Bhakti yoga, the yoga of devotion. This path is known

as the path of love and devotion. It is the path of self-surrender, of devoting and dedicating all of one's resources to attaining the ultimate reality.

Jnana yoga, the yoga of knowledge. This path involves intense discrimination. Knowledge dawns on one who persistently discriminates between the real and the unreal, between the transient and the everlasting, between the finite and the infinite. This path is tread by only a fortunate few who systematically contemplate the higher and subtler realities of life.

Kundalini yoga. There are various manuals and methods for awakening the serpent-like vital force that remains sleeping in the city of life in every human body. This is a highly technical subject for which one needs the guidance of a competent teacher.

Mantra yoga. In the deep state of meditation the highly accomplished sages in ancient times received certain sounds which are traditionally transmitted to the student, and which are to be used as objects of concentration. There are many varieties of mantras which help the student in purification, concentration, and meditation.

Hatha yoga. *Ha* and *tha* are symbolic syllables used to indicate the flow of breath in the right and left nostrils. Hatha yoga deals mostly with exercises for the body and breath which prepare the student to become aware of his internal states. Hatha yoga exercises are designed in such a way that the body becomes an instrument for treading the path of the higher life.

Raja yoga, the royal path. This highly scientific path was systematized by the codifier of yoga, Patanjali. By following it one learns to control his desires, emotions, and thoughts, as well as the subtle impressions that lie dormant in the unconscious. It unites the individual to the cosmic reality by means of the eight rungs in the ladder of yoga, which are systematically explained and described. The aspirant finally gains the eighth rung, called *samadhi*.

As emphasized earlier, these paths are not mutually exclusive. Every student of yoga practices them all to some extent, for perfection comes only when man develops his actions, speech, and mind together. One-sided development is not desirable. Karma yoga helps one to perform duties in the external world so that actions become means rather than obstacles in the path of self-realization. Bhakti yoga develops devotion and faith and destroys hindrances to concentration and meditation. It makes the aspirant into a gentle being and develops a zeal for giving. In this way relations with others become harmonious. Jnana yoga removes the veil of ignorance and develops the power of discrimination and will. Study and contemplation of the scriptures, with the aid of a competent teacher, completely and finally help one in attaining self-realization. Raja yoga steadies the mind and makes it one-pointed.

The differences between the different paths of yoga lie in the preliminary stages and in the methods of concentration they prescribe, but the final three stages of development are common to all. These are the stages of concentration, meditation, and the final union of samadhi. They all lead to the state of perfection, wisdom, and bliss.

The yoga described by Patanjali in his *Yoga Sutra* is raja yoga, the royal path. It encompasses teachings from all the different paths, and because of the variety of methods it includes, it can be practiced by people of varying backgrounds and temperaments. Raja yoga is involved with three dimensions or realms: physical, mental, and spiritual. Through its methods one achieves mastery of all three and is thus led to full realization of the Self. It is a systematic and scientific discipline that does not impose unquestioning faith, but encourages healthy discrimination. Certain practices are prescribed, along with a description of the benefits derived from them; thus raja yoga can be scientifically verified by anyone who accepts its methods as a hypothesis to be tested by his own experience. Because of this, raja yoga is ideally suited to modern times in which skepticism is almost a religion.

Raja yoga is also called ashtanga yoga, or the eightfold path, because its eight steps trace a systematic path of regulation and control from the gross (the physical body), to the subtle (the senses), to the subtlest (the manifestations of the mind). The eight steps are *yama, niyama, asana, pranayama, pratyahara, dharana, dhyana,* and *samadhi.* They will be described briefly here, and in the following chapters, each will be discussed in detail.

The first four steps—yama, niyama, asana, and pranayama— comprise the path of hatha yoga, which is both auxiliary and preliminary to the last four stages of raja yoga. Yama and niyama are the ten commitments of yoga. The five yamas, or restraints, are nonviolence, truthfulness, nonstealing, continence, and nonpossessiveness. Their practice leads to behavioral modifications in which all imperfections are replaced by virtues. The five niyamas, or observances, are cleanliness (both external and internal), contentment, practices which bring about perfection of body and senses, study of the scriptures, and surrender to the ultimate reality. The niyamas regulate one's habits and hence lead to the control of one's behavior, for actions, when repeated, crystallize into habits, and these habits, in the course of time, are incorporated as definite traits in one's personality.

The beginner should not be discouraged by the immensity of these first two steps of raja yoga. He is not asked to perfect the yamas and niyamas before proceeding further, but he should try to practice them as conscientiously as he can. With persistent effort he will eventually be able to perfect them.

When hatha yoga is taught in the West, however, usually only asanas and certain breathing exercises are taught. The yamas and niyamas are neglected because of the difficulties they entail and the lifestyle changes that are necessary in order to practice them. Hatha yoga has, therefore, degenerated into a cult of physical beauty and prolonged youth. It is true that asanas and breathing exercises ensure physical health and harmony, but their full benefits can be realized only by one whose mind is free from violent and distracting emotions. It is the yamas and niyamas that enable the student to cultivate a steady and tranquil mind.

The third step in raja yoga is asana, or posture, of which there are two types: meditative postures and postures that ensure physical well-being. A stable, meditative posture leads, in the course of time, to a stable mind, for the mind and body interact to an amazing degree. If the body is uncomfortable and unsteady it acts upon the mind, making it unsteady and distracted. Experience has shown that a posture suitable for meditation should be comfortable and stable, ensuring that the head, neck, and trunk are erect and in a straight line. Such a posture makes it possible for one to have a motionless body, thus preventing unchecked restlessness from disturbing the mind and dissipating the will. The beginner should select and cultivate one meditative posture and not change it continually.

The second kind of posture is practiced to perfect the

body, making it supple and free from disease. These postures control specific muscles and nerves and hence have therapeutic benefits. For instance, yogis have cured diseases such as leprosy with the posture called *mayurasana,* the peacock posture; the yogic posture of relaxation, called *shavasana,* in conjunction with certain breathing techniques, can cure hypertension, heart ailments, and several other imbalances of the body and mind. Specific postures and their therapeutic effects will be studied in detail in chapter three.

The fourth step of raja yoga is pranayama, or control of *prana,* the vital energy that sustains the body and mind. The grossest manifestation of prana is the breath, so pranayama is also called the science of breathing. Regulation of breath leads to regulation of the mind, for if the mind is disturbed, there is a corresponding disturbance in the breathing, and vice versa. This is easily observed in one who is afraid, excited, overcome by passion, and the like. His breathing is rapid and irregular. By the same token, continuous regulation of the breathing rhythm leads to a calm mind. In addition, the exercises of pranayama purify and strengthen the nervous system.

The fifth step of raja yoga is pratyahara, or withdrawal and control of the senses. The mind contacts the objects of the world through the five senses of sight, hearing, touch, taste, and smell. It is thus constantly gathering sensations from the external world, and these sensations set it to wandering. The student of yoga should therefore acquire the ability to voluntarily draw the senses inward and thus isolate himself from the distractions of the world outside. To do this, the student should always be aware of the sense organs and should attempt to control their activity (this is not a physical process but a voluntary, mental one), for withdrawing the senses from external objects is an essential preliminary to concentration.

Dharana, or concentration, is the sixth step in raja yoga. In concentration the dissipated powers of the mind are gathered together and directed toward the object of concentration through continued voluntary attention. Involuntary attention is effortless, but in voluntary attention a conscious effort of the will is involved. This is developed through perseverance. When the will is strengthened the student is able to concentrate, and then there is a focusing of the mind on the object of concentration, which may be an external object or a mental concept (the guru usually chooses a suitable object for concentration, based on his judgment of the student's abilities and needs). Through dharana, or concentration, the diffused mind is focused and hence made more powerful and penetrating. Therefore, in order to fulfill the latent potentials of the mind, one should systematically cultivate the ability to concentrate.

Prolonged, unbroken concentration leads to the state of dhyana, or meditation, which is the seventh step in raja yoga. Concentration makes the mind one-pointed and steady. Meditation expands the one-pointed mind to the superconscious state by piercing through its conscious and subconscious levels. Meditation is the uninterrupted flow of the mind toward one object or concept, and with this flow intuitive knowledge dawns. All methods of yoga prepare one to reach the stage of meditation, for only through meditation can one reach the level of the superconscious mind and hence attain perfection.

Why is meditation necessary? Just as there is a subconscious state beneath the conscious state, so is there a superconscious state above the conscious state. Meditation alone can take man to this blissful state of mind. Few people reach it because it is possible to get there only through persistent effort, and only after meditation has become a part of daily life.

Meditation can also help overcome physical and psychological problems. A large percentage of all diseases is psychosomatic, arising from conflicts, repressions, and suppressions in the unconscious mind. Meditation leads to an awareness of these conflicts and helps one to analyze and then erase them, thus establishing harmony at the unconscious level.

No truly intelligent person could possibly be satisfied with modern education. It is superficial and one-sided and involves repetitious parroting; it does not help one to know, develop, and control one's internal states. Meditation alone can help one to do this. Man then becomes aware of his latent powers and is able to control his subtler energies, thus becoming more creative and dynamic. In such a man the so-called supernatural powers of telepathy, clairvoyance, and the like arise spontaneously. His limitations begin to drop away, and "miracles" are within his abilities. The prophets of all religions were, through their meditative prowess, able to perform many miracles, which were not really miracles at all but only the fulfilling of the natural potential within all human beings. The training and discipline needed to reach such a state, however, ensure against the misuse of these powers for selfish ends. A wise man regards such powers merely as by-products of yogic discipline, indications of progress. His sole aim is union with the cosmic spirit, and he is not blinded by the powers. He simply continues to practice the disciplines until he reaches the state of perfection.

Prolonged and intense meditation leads to the last step of raja yoga—the state of samadhi, or the superconscious state. In this state man becomes one with the Divine and transcends all imperfections and limitations. This is the state of mystic union described in Christian, Buddhist, Muslim, and Hindu scriptures. The state of samadhi is also known as the fourth state of sleepless sleep which transcends the three normal states of waking, dreaming, and dreamless sleep. He who has attained samadhi is a blessing to society, for if humanity is to achieve a better civilization, it is possible only through the growth of the inner being. The entire life of a person who is established in samadhi is a spontaneous expression of the unhindered flow of supreme consciousness.

The physical sciences are based on sense perceptions that are interpreted by the rational faculty. Sense perceptions and rationality, however, are limited by time, space, and causation. They do not give us a complete understanding of the various forces shaping man and creation. Yoga science is the soul of all sciences and all philosophies. It can solve the basic problems of modern man, both in the East and in the West. It is definite and systematic, and it leads to the highest source of knowledge, which is called intuitive knowledge.

The teachings of yoga have been handed down to us because of the ancient yogis of India who lived selfless lives, renouncing worldly cares and pleasures in order to devote themselves to the meditative life. Their unique experiences enabled them to understand and interpret correctly the true nature of matter, mind, and energy, and this knowledge, gleaned from their intuitive experiences, was then expressed outwardly in a systematic manner. It is this direct knowledge that has been handed down from guru to disciple in a long chain from ancient times to the present day. Fortunate indeed is the sincere aspirant who comes into contact with this continuous and spontaneous flow of truth. Through these ancient teachings he can raise the capacity of his mind to perceive, assimilate, and respond to the infinite consciousness which is the basis of all manifestation.

· CHAPTER TWO ·

Yama and Niyama

THE MIND AND BODY interact to a greater extent than is normally imagined. In fact, modern scientific findings are beginning to indicate that most diseases are physical manifestations of mental and emotional disturbances. In other words, physical health is dependent on mental well-being, and it is therefore necessary to cultivate mental attitudes which ensure a steady and tranquil mind before turning one's attention to physical well-being. That is why the rungs of asana and pranayama are preceded by yama and niyama. If the mind is subject to unsettling emotions, the resulting bodily disturbances cannot be combated by any of the known asanas. The value of asanas and pranayama is therefore limited unless they are taught in conjunction with the yamas and niyamas, the moral code, or ten commitments, of raja yoga.

Yama

The yamas are the five restraints that regulate one's relationship with other beings. They are: *ahimsa,* nonviolence;

satya, truthfulness; *asteya,* nonstealing; *brahmacharya,* abstinence from sensual indulgence; *aparigraha,* nonpossessiveness.

Ahimsa literally means "nonhurting or nonviolence." One normally thinks of violence only in terms of the physical, and most people in civilized societies refrain from gross acts of physical violence. Ahimsa, however, refers to nonviolence in thought and word as well as in deed. Violence in speech or in action is almost always preceded by violent thoughts, and violent thoughts have serious repercussions on the mind and on the body—they should be avoided, if only for this reason. On the positive side, careful cultivation of ahimsa leads to a spontaneous, all-encompassing love. One begins to see the unity in all creation and thus progresses toward the goal of self-realization.

Satya, or truthfulness, is an essential part of all codes of morality in all societies. One should be truthful to oneself and to others in thought, word, and deed. As most people know, one lie inevitably leads to another, and soon deception becomes second nature, leading to a fearful and scheming mind. It is said that if a person makes truth the central focus of his life, all of his utterances will come true, for such a person is incapable of untruth.

Asteya, or nonstealing, includes refraining from misappropriation, accepting bribes, and the like. The desire for what another owns can be very strong, for the mind, when possessed by it, is capable of little else. Such an attitude of mind is based on underlying feelings of inadequacy and jealousy, a sense of having been cheated, and a desire for retribution. One is haunted by the thought that "someone else has what I need in order to feel complete and fulfilled." But stealing an external object does not get rid of the basic sense of inadequacy, so one surreptitiously takes, again and again. Still, the underlying feelings remain. Cultivating asteya counteracts such attitudes. It helps to develop a sense of completeness and self-sufficiency and leads to freedom from the bondage of such cravings.

Brahmacharya literally means "to walk in Brahman." One who cultivates this yama is aware of Brahman alone. Such a state is possible only if the mind is free from all sensual desires. The sexual urge is the most powerful and the most destructive of all sensual desires. Brahmacharya is therefore often translated as abstinence from sex, or celibacy. In reality, it refers to continence in either the celibate or the married state, for sexual excess leads to the dissipation of vital energy that could be used instead to attain deeper states of consciousness. Brahmacharya should not, however, be interpreted as repression of sensual urges—repression leads only to frustration and an abnormal state of mind. Brahmacharya means control of and freedom from all sensual cravings. The bliss that accompanies self-realization is far greater than any transient sensual pleasure, and one whose goal is self-realization would therefore overcome the obstacles of sensual cravings without any kind of suppression.

Aparigraha, or nonpossessiveness, has been misunderstood to mean denying oneself all material possessions. But as is the case with each of these restraints, this practice fosters an inward attunement rather than an outward appearance. It involves not being addicted to, or dependent on, one's possessions rather than the outward denial of them. A beggar, for instance, could be more attached to his begging bowl than a king to all his treasures. The danger lies not in having material possessions; it lies in becoming attached to them or in craving more.

Niyama

The niyamas are the observances one should follow. They are five in number: *shaucha,* purity; *santosha,* contentment; *tapas,* practices that lead to perfection of body, mind, and senses; *svadhyaya,* study that leads to knowledge of the Self; and *Ishvara-pranidhana,* surrender to the ultimate reality.

Shaucha involves purity, both of the body and the mind. Purity of the body is easily achieved, but not purity of the mind. To achieve this state one should cultivate *smriti,* mindfulness, and *buddhi,* discrimination. That is, one should always be aware of one's thoughts and should learn to discriminate between pure and impure thoughts on the basis of whether they lead to greater freedom or to greater bondage and ignorance. Sincerity and perseverance are essential in cultivating this niyama.

Santosha, or contentment, is a state of mind which is not dependent on one's material status. A beggar, for instance, can be as content as a king, if not more so. Man's desires are insatiable, and no sooner is one fulfilled than another arises. The mind is therefore in a constant state of agitation, and tranquility is possible only through the cultivation of santosha. But contentment should not lead to slackening of effort. Rather, effort should stem from a sense of duty and service instead of from discontent or anticipation of the fruits of one's efforts.

Tapas has often been wrongly interpreted as excessive austerity and mortification of the flesh, as exemplified by the hair shirt and bed of nails. But in the Bhagavad Gita, Lord Krishna clearly states that yoga is not for the person who indulges the flesh nor for the person who tortures it. *Tapas* literally means "that which generates heat," for heat arises in a person who is full of spiritual fervor and has a burning zeal for enlightenment. Acts which increase this spiritual fervor constitute tapas. So a simple life, free from sensual indulgence and including regulated fasting, chanting the name of the Lord, and serving one's fellowmen, all constitute tapas. Through tapas one develops strength of body and mind, and the blaze of spiritual fervor burns brighter.

Svadhyaya is study leading to knowledge of the Self. This begins with intellectual pursuits—understanding the scriptures and other books of spiritual value. Rational acceptance of spiritual truths leads, upon further reflection and meditation, to intuitive insights and then to the true understanding of these truths, which is supported by study of the internal states of consciousness. Only then does knowledge of the Self begin to dawn on the aspirant.

Ishvara-pranidhana, or surrender to the ultimate reality, is possible only with infinite faith and dedication. This is total surrender and is achieved only through time, sincerity, and perseverance. The ego has great tenacity and resists such complete surrender, but when it is transcended, knowledge of one's true nature is attained.

An aspirant could easily be overwhelmed by the immensity of the task of applying the yamas and niyamas to daily life. The initial step might seem so difficult that one would despair of ever being able to progress further. The aspirant is not, however, asked to attain perfection in the yamas and niyamas right away. Few would be capable of this. Instead, regard the yamas and niyamas as ideals toward which an aspirant works with sincerity. In the meantime, attempt to observe them to the fullest extent possible. Each failure should be motivation for future success, while even a small degree of success will reduce the intensity of emotional upheavals and mental distractions.

· CHAPTER THREE ·

Asanas and Their Therapeutic Value

PATANJALI HAS NOT described asana and pranayama in detail. These aspects of raja yoga were developed later by the exponents of hatha yoga who realized that in order to arouse kundalini, the latent energy within, one has to practice and perfect asanas and pranayama, for a sickly and dissipated constitution is an obstacle when one scales the higher rungs of the yoga ladder. Hatha yoga is therefore necessary to ensure physical health and harmony—prerequisites for concentration and meditation. It is both an auxiliary to raja yoga and an essential part of it.

Asana is the Sanskrit word for posture, of which there are two kinds—asanas for meditation and asanas for physical well-being. The asanas suitable for pranayama, concentration, and meditation are *padmasana,* the lotus posture; *siddhasana,* the accomplished posture; *svastikasana,* the auspicious posture; *sukhasana,* the easy posture; and a few others. In all of them, emphasis is placed on keeping the head, neck, and trunk erect, which results in a steady and comfortable posture with minimal retention of carbon dioxide.

This slows down the activity of the heart and lungs; as a result, the mind is less disturbed by the body. This in turn aids concentration greatly. The other asanas, which aim at physical well-being, control specific muscles, nerves, and glands in the body and have specific therapeutic effects.

Photographs of some of the more important asanas are included in this book, but there is no detailed discussion of their practice or of the precautionary measures to be observed. Consult a manual on hatha yoga for this purpose; personal instruction from a competent teacher is necessary in the more advanced postures. In this chapter we will consider the physiological aspects of some of the asanas for physical well-being and their value as therapeutic measures, but first we will examine those postures used for practicing meditation and pranayama.

Meditative Postures

Patanjali's *Yoga Sutra*, as well as other scriptures, places great emphasis on cultivating a posture that is comfortable and steady, one in which the head, neck, and trunk are erect and in line. If in the early stages the aspirant does not heed this injunction and assumes his own posture for concentration and meditation, he will suffer from a serious handicap when trying to scale the higher rungs of the yoga ladder. Those who want to tread the path of yoga seriously and successfully should follow the order and the scientific process expounded by experienced yogis. If the head, neck, and trunk are not erect, the aspirant's body begins to tremble after a few minutes, disturbing his mind. The trunk slowly begins to curve, restricting the flow of vital energy through the spinal cord, and causing the gland centers to be deprived of the energizing circulation of blood. Finally, improper and restricted blood circulation upsets the respiratory system, and the aspirant will find it difficult to breathe in a natural way. In order to prevent these problems the adepts of ancient wisdom have formulated four main postures for practicing the science of breath, concentration, and meditation.

The Lotus Posture *(Padmasana)*

Sit on the floor on a rug or a blanket that has been folded a few times to provide a cushion, and spread the legs forward. Now bring the head, neck, and trunk into a straight line. Slowly lift the left foot with the hands and place it on the right thigh. Then place the right foot on the left thigh. Place the hands on the knees, with the tips of the index finger and thumb joined to form a circle. Or you may place the hands on the knees palms upward, with the tip of the index finger touching the midportion of the thumb (Fig. 1).

If the lotus posture is uncomfortable or painful, the aspirant can try one of the other postures instead. The lotus is used mainly in order to develop limberness in the lower extremities, but it is not ordinarily used as a meditative posture. Highly accomplished yogis usually master *siddhasana*. Only a few adepts master *padmasana,* because it is difficult to apply the root lock in this posture.

The Accomplished Posture *(Siddhasana)*

In *siddhasana* (Fig. 2), the left heel is placed at the perineum (the region between the anus and the genitals) after the root lock has been applied. (This is done by contracting the anal sphincter muscles and pulling them in.) Now the other heel is placed at the pubic bone above the organ of generation. The feet and legs are arranged so that the ankle

Fig. 1 Lotus Posture *(Padmasana)*

Fig. 2 Accomplished Posture *(Siddhasana)*

joints are in one line, or touch each other. The toes of the right foot are placed between the left thigh and calf so that only the big toe is visible, and the toes of the left foot are pulled up between the right thigh and calf so that the big toe is visible. The hands may then be placed as in the lotus.

The Auspicious Posture *(Svastikasana)*

This posture (Fig. 3) is a comfortable one and is especially recommended for women. It is similar to the accomplished posture except that the heels and ankle bones are not aligned. The left leg is bent at the knee and the left foot is placed with the sole in close contact with the right thigh. The right foot is then placed on top of the left calf, with the outer edge of the foot and the toes between the thigh and

Fig. 3 Auspicious Posture *(Svastikasana)*

calf muscles. Only the big toe should be visible. The toes of the left foot are then pulled up between the right thigh and calf so that the big toe is visible. In this way a symmetrical and stable posture is attained. The hands may be arranged as in the first two postures.

The Easy Posture (Sukhasana)

This simple cross-legged posture (Fig. 4) can be used if the other three postures are painful or uncomfortable. It may also be used by beginners and older individuals. Here, the left foot is placed below the right knee and the right foot just below the left knee. Each knee can then rest on the opposite foot.

Fig. 4 Easy Posture (Sukhasana)

After mastering one of these four postures the aspirant will experience great joy in it. If there is pain in the legs after sitting in the posture for awhile, stretch the legs, massage them for a few minutes, and then resume the posture. It is quite permissible for beginners, or those who experience difficulty sitting in the time-honored postures, to sit erect in a straight-backed chair, placing the hands on the knees or thighs, and keeping the head, neck, and trunk straight. Do not keep changing your meditation posture; choose one and practice it regularly. Through continual practice of a steady posture mastery over the body and mind is acquired.

Postures for Physical Well-being

Asanas should be performed on a carpet or folded blanket in a clean, quiet, well-ventilated room or in the open air. They may be performed in the morning or in the evening (the body is more flexible in the evening). A warm bath beforehand is helpful, as it promotes circulation and reduces stiffness of the joints. The bladder and bowels must be emptied before practicing asanas, and at least four hours should have elapsed since the last normal-sized meal. All movements should be slow, deliberate, and controlled. Asanas should be performed only to the extent that is comfortable; overstraining should be avoided. Patience, perseverance, and regularity ensure success.

A consideration of the internal workings of the body reveals that the nervous, endocrine, circulatory, digestive, urinary, and respiratory systems are especially significant to physical well-being. The nervous system coordinates the functions of all the other systems in the body. The endocrine glands influence the nervous system and also help in maintaining the physiological balance of the different organs. The circulatory system is responsible for transporting nourishment to all the cells of the body and for carrying waste products away from the cells. In addition, the blood cells carry wastes away; absorb proteins, fats, sugars, and salts from digested food in the stomach and intestines; and absorb oxygen from the inhaled air in the lungs. The air exhaled by the lungs carries away carbon dioxide from the blood cells, while other waste products are eliminated as feces through the colon and as urine through the urinary system. Thus these different systems work together to maintain physical health. We will now consider the beneficial influence of the asanas on these biological systems.

The Headstand *(Shirshasana)*

Because the headstand (Fig. 5) is an inverted posture, it brings a rich supply of arterial blood to the brain, cranial nerves, and pituitary and pineal glands. It also provides efficient drainage of venous blood from the legs and abdominal cavity back to the heart. Therefore the brain, nervous system, pituitary and pineal glands, digestive organs, and veins in the legs benefit from this asana. It promotes general well-being and may be used to relieve cases of nervous debility, dyspepsia and constipation, seminal weakness, and varicose veins.

1. Sitting on the heels, bend forward, placing the forearms on the floor. The elbows should be near, or a few inches ahead of, the knees. Position the elbows slightly less than a shoulder's width apart. The proper distance can be found by bringing the knees together and placing the elbows on the outside of each knee or by enclosing each hand around the opposite elbow. Interlock the fingers, forming a cup with the hands.

Fig. 5 Headstand *(Shirshasana)*

2. Place the front of the top of the head, at about the
   hairline, on the floor (make sure the floor is well-
   cushioned). Rest the back of the head in the hands.
   Slowly walk the feet toward the body and bring the
   knees to the chest.

3. Inhaling, raise both feet off the floor, keeping the knees to the chest in a tucked position. Become balanced and steady at this point.

4. Keeping the knees bent, slowly raise the thighs away from the chest, bringing them up and aligning them with the trunk, letting the lower legs and feet remain limp.

5. Straighten the legs, keeping the heels together, pointing the toes upward. The weight of the body is borne by the head, forearms, and elbows. Pulling in the stomach will prevent the back from arching.

6. Become steady in the pose, concentrating on breathing evenly and achieving balance.

7. Hold the pose to your capacity, increasing up to five minutes for full benefit; then come down slowly, retracing all the steps.

   Relax in the child's pose by sitting back on the heels with the forehead on the floor and the arms alongside the body.

The Shoulderstand *(Sarvangasana)*

The shoulderstand (Fig. 6) stimulates the thyroid and parathyroid glands and maintains them in a healthy condition. The thyroid gland influences the functions of the whole system, so this asana promotes health throughout the entire body. That is why it is called *sarvangasana* (sarva in Sanskrit means "all" and *anga* means "limb"). In this asana the flood of blood to the brain is checked because the chin is pressed against the chest and, as in the headstand, there is easy drainage of venous blood from the legs and abdominal cavity. This asana may be used to relieve nervous debility,

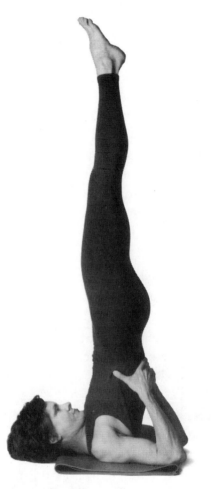

Fig. 6 Shoulderstand *(Sarvangasana)*

dyspepsia and constipation, degeneration of the sex glands, hypertension, hemorrhoids, varicose veins, bronchitis, headaches, throat ailments, and many other common problems. It also helps to rejuvenate the whole body and to combat the effects of old age.

1. Lie down on the back, arms at the sides, palms down, and feet together.

2. Exhale, slowly raising both legs until they are perpendicular to the floor. Lift the hips off the floor and bring the feet toward the floor behind the head. The chest should meet the chin to form a chin lock.

3. Place the palms as high up on the back as possible, fingers toward the center of the back, keeping the elbows as close together as possible (not more than shoulder-width apart).

4. Exhaling, raise both legs until they are in line with the toes.

5. Keep the legs straight by tightening the hamstrings and buttock muscles. Keep the stomach pulled in. The whole body should be straight and perpendicular to the floor.

6. Hold to your capacity. In order to gain the full benefits of the posture, hold it for five minutes.

7. Lower the arms to the floor, palms down. Then slowly lower the back to the floor, one vertebra at a time.

8. Inhale and lower the legs to the floor.

9. Relax and breathe deeply, lying flat on the back.

The Fish Posture (Matsyasana)

This asana (Fig. 7) is complementary to the shoulderstand and always follows it. Only then does one achieve the full benefit of the shoulderstand. *Matsyasana* also stimulates the thyroid and parathyroid glands; it eliminates stiffness in the neck and back and increases blood circulation to the face and neck. Since the chest is expanded, breathing becomes

Fig. 7 Fish Posture *(Matsyasana)*

fuller. The pelvic joints also become more flexible. This asana is used to relieve common colds and inflamed tonsils as well as inflamed and bleeding hemorrhoids.

1. Assume the lotus posture.

2. Lie on the back; do not allow the knees to be raised from the floor.

3. Exhale completely; then, inhaling, rise up on the elbows, lifting the chest and head from the floor. Allow the head to fall backward until the top of the head rests on the floor. Keeping the upper back arched and the chest expanded, allow the weight of the trunk to rest on the top of the head, stretching the neck. The hands may take hold of the toes. Breathe deeply.

4. To come out of the pose, support the body with the elbows. With an exhalation, loosen the pressure on the head and neck, lowering yourself completely to the floor.

5. Relax and breathe deeply, lying flat on the back.

The Plow Posture *(Halasana)*

This posture (Fig. 8) is a great benefit to the spine and spinal nerves—and a youthful spine makes the body youthful. The plow also stimulates the thyroid and parathyroid glands (though to a lesser extent than the shoulderstand) and contracts the abdominal muscles, strengthening the digestive system. This asana may be used to correct deviations of the spine; combat constipation; help arthritis of the back; rejuvenate the digestive organs, sex glands, and kidneys; alleviate headaches; and eliminate fatigue.

1. Lie on the back, feet together and palms on the floor.
2. Slowly raise the legs until they are perpendicular to the floor. Lift the trunk, and keeping the legs straight and close together, lower the toes to the floor as close to the head as possible. All movements should be performed slowly and gracefully.

Fig. 8 Plow Posture *(Halasana)*

3. After this position has been maintained for a few seconds, the toes should be pushed further beyond the head, feeling pressure first at the lower dorsal region, then at the upper dorsal region, and last in the cervical region when the pose is fully extended. This position presses the chin tightly to form a perfect chin lock.

4. Place the arms over the head, fingers pointing toward the toes, and breathe deeply.

5. Return the toes again to their original position near the head. Maintain the pose twenty to thirty seconds in this position. Then retrace all the steps in coming out of the pose. Relax.

6. Relax and breathe deeply, lying flat on the back.

The Cobra Posture *(Bhujangasana)*
The Locust Posture *(Shalabhasana)*
The Bow Posture *(Dhanurasana)*

These three postures (Figs. 9, 10, and 11) have been grouped together because they all give the spine a backward bend and stretch the abdominal muscles. In the cobra, and to a lesser extent in the bow, the deep muscles of the back are exercised, promoting blood circulation to the back muscles, spine and spinal nerves, and abdominal organs. The chest is also expanded in these asanas, so breathing becomes fuller. The locust requires retention of the breath, and the resulting pressure in the lungs helps in maintaining their elasticity. These asanas also prevent functional disturbances of the stomach, liver, kidneys, and intestines, and may be used to combat constipation, lumbago, gastric trouble, flatulence, and backaches. The locust and bow postures may also be used to correct deviations of the spine and slipped discs.

Fig. 9 Cobra Posture (Bhujangasana)

The Cobra Posture (Bhujangasana)

1. Lie on the stomach, forehead on the floor.
2. Place the palms on the floor alongside the breasts, keeping the elbows close to the body. The toes point away from the body, with the heels together.
3. With an inhalation, slowly raise the head, then the neck and chest, one vertebra at a time, using only the muscles of the back. Keep the navel on the floor (the abdominal muscles will press into the floor). The legs should be relaxed, heels together. The arms should not bear any weight; only the lower back muscles should be used to raise and hold the pose.
4. Hold to your capacity.
5. With an exhalation, slowly lower the chest to the floor, one vertebra at a time.
6. Turn the head to one side and relax with deep, even breathing.

Fig. 10 Locust Posture *(Shalabhasana)*

The Locust Posture *(Shalabhasana)*

1. Lie on the stomach, resting the chin on the floor. The toes are pointing away from the body, heels together. Arms are at the sides, palms up.

2. Make a fist and position the hands either alongside, or just underneath, the thighs.

3. Inhale, and slowly raise both legs off the floor, keeping them straight. Then, in the same motion, tense the arms, pressing the forearms into the floor, thus raising the navel off the floor and lifting the legs still higher.

4. Hold as long as the breath can be comfortably retained.

5. Exhale, and slowly lower the legs to the floor.

6. Relax with deep, even breathing.

The Bow Posture *(Dhanurasana)*

1. Lie on the stomach; rest the chin on the floor and the arms at the sides.
2. Bend the legs at the knees and bring the heels close to the buttocks.
3. Reach back and grasp the right ankle with the right hand and the left ankle with the left hand.
4. Inhale and retain the breath, raising the chin, head, and chest while simultaneously raising the thighs and hips. Keeping the knees together, try to straighten the legs without releasing the hands. The whole body stretches up, resting on the abdomen.
5. Hold for as long as the breath can be comfortably retained.

Fig. 11 Bow Posture *(Dhanurasana)*

6. Exhaling, slowly lower the body to the floor and release the ankles.

After the cobra, locust, and bow postures, relax in the child's pose by sitting on the heels with the forehead on the floor and the arms alongside the body.

The Half Spinal Twist *(Ardha Matsyendrasana)*

This posture (Fig. 12) is useful as a spinal exercise because it gives a sideways twist to the spine in both directions. It has a beneficial effect on the whole nervous system, improves blood circulation to the abdominal organs, and strengthens the abdominal muscles. The half spinal twist may be used to relieve lumbago, displaced shoulder joints, sprains in the neck and shoulder muscles, a congested liver, a congested spleen, and inactive kidneys.

Fig. 12 Half Spinal Twist *(Ardha Matsyendrasana)*

1. Sit on the floor with the legs stretched out in front of you. Bend the right leg at the knee and place the heel against the perineum.

2. Bending the left leg, raise the knee up and cross the left foot over the right thigh, placing it firmly on the floor, the ankle against the knee.

3. Inhale and stretch the ribs up. Turn the trunk to the left. Raise the right arm over the left knee and bring the chest against the left thigh. The back of the shoulder and upper arm will press against the left knee and thigh. Place the left arm on the floor behind the left hip for balance.

4. Inhaling and twisting still more, grasp the instep of the left foot with the right hand and push the left knee further to the right. Turn the head, bringing the chin almost in line with the left shoulder. Reach across the back with the left arm and hold the right thigh just below the hip joint.

5. Breathe deeply, holding the posture to your capacity; then repeat the process on the opposite side.

6. Relax with even breathing.

The Peacock Posture (Mayurasana)

This asana (Fig. 13) strengthens the forearms, wrists, and elbows, and provides a liberal blood supply to the digestive organs. It also increases intra-abdominal pressure, thus benefiting the digestive organs and stimulating the nerves of the abdominal cavity. The peacock also helps to eliminate toxins in the body and combats ailments of the stomach, spleen, and pancreas.

1. Sit on the heels and spread the knees apart. Place the

Fig. 13 Peacock Posture *(Mayurasana)*

palms on the floor between the legs, elbows together, thumbs out, fingers extended and pointing back. Bring the forearms together from the wrists to the elbows, providing a fulcrum on which to support the body. Press the elbows against the abdomen at the navel.

2. Bend forward, placing the forehead on the floor. Straighten the legs out behind, bringing the weight of the body onto the arms and elbows.

3 Inhale, and gently come slightly forward onto the elbows, tightening the abdominal muscles and at the same time arching the lower back and raising the legs from the floor. The forearms are at a right angle to the floor and inclined slightly to the front. The head is raised and the chin thrown out to counterbalance the weight of the legs. In this position the body is held like a bar resting on a fulcrum, perfectly straight and parallel to the floor.

4. Retain the breath, and hold to your capacity.

5. Exhaling, lower the forehead to the floor. Bring the legs back underneath you and sit on the heels.

6. Relax with even breathing.

The Posterior Stretch *(Paschimottanasana)*

This posture (Fig. 14) stretches the muscles of the back and the hamstring muscles at the back of the knees. The front abdominal muscles are contracted, the pelvic and lumbosacral nerves are benefited, the spine is rendered supple, and the heart is massaged. This asana may be used to relieve malfunctioning of the stomach, liver, kidneys, and intestines, and disorders of the sex glands.

1. Sit on the floor with the legs together stretched out in front of you.

2. Inhaling, stretch the arms overhead, pulling the spine straight up. The palms should face forward.

3. Exhaling, bend forward at the hip joints (not at the waist).

Fig. 14 Posterior Stretch *(Paschimottanasana)*

4. Keeping the spine straight, grasp the toes, ankles, or calves, according to your capacity. Keep the legs straight and the back part of the knees flat on the floor. Try to stretch down until the chest and stomach lie on the thighs, and the forehead, nose, or chin rests on the knees.

5. Catch hold of the toes with the arms slightly bent and the elbows touching the floor alongside the legs; do not use the arms to pull you forward. Use the weight of the trunk to press the legs against the floor.

6. Hold to your capacity with even breathing, relaxing into the posture.

7. With an inhalation, return to the starting position.

8. Relax completely with deep, even breathing.

The Symbol of Yoga (Yoga Mudra)

This asana (Fig. 15) has many of the benefits of the posterior stretch. The pressure of the heels against the cecum and pelvic loop helps to reposition displaced abdominal organs. Yoga mudra expands the chest and increases the range of shoulder movements. Peristaltic activity is intensified. This asana is helpful for constipation and seminal weakness.

1. Assume the lotus posture. If this is not possible, either the half lotus or easy posture is acceptable. Reach behind the back with both hands, interlacing the fingers. Keep the spine erect.

2. Exhaling, bend forward from the hip joints and keep the back straight. Rest the forehead on the floor in front of the legs. Do not allow the buttocks to lift off the floor. Let the breath become deep and even, holding the pose to your capacity.

Fig. 15 The Symbol of Yoga *(Yoga Mudra)*

3. With an inhalation, and keeping the trunk straight, return to a sitting position. Release the hands and stretch the legs.

4. Relax, breathing deeply and evenly.

The Wheel Posture *(Chakrasana)*

Through this asana (Fig. 16) the body becomes supple and alert. The arms and wrists are strengthened, and the muscles of the legs, hips, and shoulders, as well as the ligaments of the spine, are stretched.

1. Lie on the back, feet slightly apart. Bend the knees and rest the spine flat on the floor. Place the hands on the floor next to the head, palms down, thumb side toward the head, with the fingers pointing toward the toes.

2. Inhaling, lift the body and rest on the top of the head, then straighten the arms and arch the back. Walk the feet toward the head but do not come up onto the toes. Push the abdomen upward and gaze at the floor between the hands. The closer the feet are to the hands, the greater the curve of the back.

Fig. 16 Wheel Posture *(Chakrasana)*

3. Breathe deeply, holding the pose to your capacity. Then, exhaling, slowly lower the body to the floor.

4. Relax in the corpse posture.

The Camel Posture *(Ustrasana)*

This posture (Fig. 17) stretches and tones the spine and is helpful for drooping shoulders and a hunched back.

1. Sit on the heels with the knees together and the back straight. Reach back and place the palms of the hands on the soles of the feet.

2. Inhaling, and without losing the contact between the hands and feet, lift the buttocks off the heels and lift the hips as far up and forward as possible. Drop the

Fig. 17 Camel Posture *(Ustrasana)*

head back and gaze at the point between the eyebrows, or close the eyes. If possible, move the hands
from the feet and grasp the ankles.

3. There is a tendency to hold the breath (as in all backward bending postures), so make an effort to breathe
deeply.

4. Return to a sitting position and relax.

The Bridge Posture *(Setu Bandhasana)*

This asana (Fig. 18) strengthens the neck as well as the
extensor muscles of the back and spine. In addition, the
pineal, pituitary, thyroid, and adrenal glands are benefited
by the increased supply of blood.

Fig. 18 Bridge Posture *(Setu Bandhasana)*

1. Lie on the back. Bring the feet to the buttocks, with the knees up, and grasp the ankles, keeping the knees and ankles together and the feet flat on the floor.

2. Inhaling, lift the hips from the floor and arch the back up, stretching the front of the thighs and contracting the buttocks. The shoulders and head should remain on the floor.

3. Hold to your capacity and breathe deeply and evenly.

4. Exhale, and lower the hips to the floor. Release the ankles, stretch the legs out straight, and relax in the corpse posture.

The Corpse Posture *(Shavasana)*

This asana (Fig. 19) relaxes the entire body. It is used in between the different asanas and after all of them have been performed. This posture reduces all muscle tension, improves venous circulation, tones the whole nervous system, and relieves fatigue. In addition, the heart is rested and the distribution of blood is uniform. The breathing becomes

Fig. 19 Corpse Posture *(Shavasana)*

slow, deep, and rhythmic. This asana is used to cure degeneration of the nerves as well as high blood pressure.

1. Lie on the back. Spread the feet apart slightly and place the arms out at the sides, palms up. Do not allow one limb to touch another. Close the eyes.
2. Relax all the muscles of the body. Let the body and mind be perfectly still. Breathe from the diaphragm—slowly and deeply. Be both mentally alert and relaxed.

The essential difference between asanas and other systems of physical culture should now be evident. While other systems aim at merely developing a muscular body, hatha yoga aims at promoting the health of the internal organs as well. Thus, complete physical harmony is achieved, which is an essential prerequisite to achieving one-pointedness of mind. But the main reason hatha yoga is important is that it is preparatory training for ascending the higher rungs of the yoga ladder.

Internal Cleansing

In addition to the postures, a number of *kriyas,* or cleansing exercises, are employed in hatha yoga. *Kriya* means "preliminary or preparatory." These techniques free the body of excess mucus and other wastes, leaving the practitioner refreshed and purified. Thus they prepare the student for the practice of meditation. Although the idea of cleaning the interior of the body may not be appealing at first, once the student experiences the sense of invigoration and feeling of lightness that it brings, and experiences the freedom from colds and chronic ailments that can result, he begins to take pleasure in them. To the practitioner who has refined his sensitivity to internal processes, the practices of internal cleansing become as important as bathing is to most people.

A few of the most basic kriyas will be described. They should be practiced in the morning, shortly after arising, before doing asanas and before eating.

Nasal Wash *(Jala Neti)*

This is a technique for removing excess mucus from the nasal and sinus passages. It clears obstructions so that the breath can flow freely through the nostrils. This helps prevent colds and relieves the symptoms of hay fever and other allergies. Variations of this practice are now recommended by some physicians.

1. Place half a cup of tepid water into a small vessel which has an extended spout. Add a pinch (approximately one-fourth teaspoon) of salt to the water. The proper amount of salt should produce a solution which tastes like tears. This degree of saltiness has a soothing effect on the lining of the nose and throat,

Fig. 20 Nasal Wash *(Jala Neti)*

and will prevent the water from causing a burning sensation in the nasal passages.

2. Stand over a sink and tilt the head to the right. Place the spout against the left nostril and slowly pour in the water. If the head is tilted at the proper angle the water will run out the opposite nostril (Fig. 20).

3. Repeat the same procedure on the other side, pouring the water into the right nostril.

4. Remove excess water from the nasal passages by bending over until the head is upside down and then tilting the head.

String Cleansing *(Sutra Neti)*

In this practice, a length of good quality, sterilized cotton cord is used to clean the nasal passages. In addition to removing excess mucus and keeping the nostrils free of obstruction, this practice facilitates the proper flow of air and thereby makes the breathing exercises easier. It decreases the likelihood of developing ailments of the upper respiratory passages as well, and improves such conditions as sinusitis and weak vision.

1. A length of quality sterilized cotton cord is unraveled on one end, and the other end is dipped in beeswax. As this end stiffens it should be made blunt.

2. Insert the blunt end gently into the nostril several inches so that it enters the passage coming down toward the throat. (During the first few attempts, tears and sneezing may be induced; this subsides with practice.)

3. When the end of the string is felt at the base of the tongue, reach inside the mouth with the thumb and index finger, grasping the blunt end and pulling it out through the mouth. The other end remains in the nostril.

4. Move the string back and forth slowly, gently cleaning the nasal passage.

5. Remove the string and repeat the process in the other nostril.

Upper Wash (Gajakarani)

The upper wash is an exercise that cleans the stomach and bronchial passages. It is performed by swallowing a large quantity of water, then regurgitating it. The upward pressure not only empties the stomach, it also forces accumulated mucus out of the respiratory passages. It has been proven to alleviate some respiratory diseases as well as some gastric disorders.

1. The stomach should be empty (unless the kriya is per-

formed to clear the digestive tract of undesirable food).

2. Prepare four to six quarts of lukewarm water and add enough salt to make it taste somewhat stronger than tears.

3. In a squatting position, drink the water as rapidly as possible, with no pause or interruption.

4. By the time this amount of water has been swallowed, regurgitation will often occur spontaneously. If not, stand up, lean forward over a basin, insert the fingers in the throat and gently stimulate the back of the tongue, simultaneously pushing and massaging the upper abdomen with the other hand. Be careful not to scratch or injure the throat with the fingernails.

5. All the water should be thrown up. When first performing the exercise it is helpful to measure the amount of water taken in as well as that thrown up.

6. Afterward, take only juices for several hours. A heavy meal should not be taken for some time.

Cleansing with a Cloth *(Dhauti)*

This practice removes excess mucus from the esophagus and stomach, where it tends to accumulate as a result of the constant swallowing of drainage from the sinuses, nasal passages, and bronchi.

1. Use a three-inch wide strip of very fine white cotton cloth, 22 to 23 feet in length for this practice (the beginner may use a shorter cloth).

2. Sterilize the cloth by boiling it in water.

3. Grasp one end of the cloth, spreading it out and placing it as far back on the tongue as possible.

4. Begin swallowing the cloth as you continue to spread it and feed it into the mouth. If the cloth does not go down, swallowing a few sips of water will often help to get it started.

5. Continue swallowing until you are holding only six inches of the cloth outside the mouth.

6. Pull the cloth out rapidly, allowing the natural gag reflex to help expel both it and the accompanying mucus.

· CHAPTER FOUR ·

Pranayama

WHEN A STUDENT starts practicing postures accurately he becomes more aware of variations in the flow of his breath, and then the teacher can begin to give him various breathing techniques or pranayama practices. The meaning of the word *pranayama* may be explained in two ways. *Prana* is "energy or life force" and *yama* is "the control of that energy." Or the word may be divided into *prana* and *ayama. Ayama* means "expansion or rising," so pranayama may be understood as the practice whereby the flow of prana is made more extensive and expansive.

The word *prana* itself is composed of two words, *pra* and *na. Pra* means "first unit" and na means "energy." This first unit of energy exists in its subtlest aspect in man; the universe is its expansion. Thus there is no qualitative difference between man and the universe. The underlying principle in both is prana, for prana is the sum total of all energy that is manifest in man and the universe. In the beginning there was *akasha,* or empty space alone, but through prana the universe manifested. All that is present in the world of sense perception is only an expression of this vital energy. It is prana that feeds and sustains the mind and produces thoughts. It is therefore related to the mind, through mind to the will, through will to the individual soul, *Atman,* and thus to the cosmic soul, *Brahman.* All sensations, all thinking, feeling, and knowing are possible only because of prana.

The science of breath is an important part of the science of pranayama, but the world has not yet recognized the importance of the science of breath. Yogis alone know the secret of this science, for the subject is vast and recondite. Many talk of physical health. Others talk of the soul, the universe, and God. But the real mystery of prana remains veiled even though it is prana that sustains the body. Without its help the body and mind could not exist.

Modern science has done much research on diet, calories, vitamins, and minerals. The mind and its functions are also being studied. But it is the breath that links the body and mind, and very little research has been focused here. There are many books on philosophy and religion, but few books deal with pranayama because it must be known experientially. Only one who has mastered its practices can explain it thoroughly.

Prana sustains life. It enters the body through the food we eat and the air we breathe. The vital part of food is prana, without which none can live, but food contains a grosser quality of prana than does the breath, which carries it in a more subtle form. In other words, the vital energy contained in the food we eat is important, but even more indispensable is the vital energy contained in the air we breathe. There is no medicine known to man which can substitute for this vital energy. It is important to remember, though, that prana is not the air or the food itself; they are merely vehicles for its subtle energy. So just as man takes in vitamins, protein, and calories, he should also learn the most important exercise of filling his lungs completely at least twice a day.

Regulating the lungs is the most vital process in cleansing the human system. When our lungs go into action, an exchange takes place between the prana that is about to be consumed and that prana that has already been consumed. Overeating or eating overcooked food disrupts this exchange, and the lungs as well as the entire respiratory system become irregular. Even the pores suffer. When we regulate the motion of the lungs by certain breathing exercises, however, the pores function properly and the tissues and cells become healthy.

The lungs are situated on each side of the chest, with the heart, great vessels, and esophagus separating them and the air passages leading to them. At the base of the lungs we find the diaphragm, the muscular wall dividing the chest cavity from the abdomen. It is the action of the diaphragm which draws air into the lungs. The diaphragm contracts, pulling air into the lungs. When the diaphragm relaxes, the lungs contract and the air is expelled. So control of the diaphragm is the first step in the practice of breathing exercises. The simple practice of deep breathing with diaphragmatic movement is the foundation of the science of breath.

The air we inhale helps all the systems in our body perform their respective functions. In controlling the motion of our lungs, we are regulating the exchange in the storehouse of vital energies. Furthermore, by controlling the motion of their lungs, highly accomplished yogis can control their autonomic nervous system and the muscles associated with it. The functioning of prana is the basic principle underlying the systolic and diastolic action of the heart; the exhalation and inhalation of the lungs; the digestion of food; the excretion of urine and fecal matter; and the manufacture of gastric juice, bile, intestinal juice, and saliva.

By controlling the motion of the lungs one can also control the functioning of the pores: the pores play a crucial part in cleansing the whole body. A yoga manual, the *Tarangini*, explains a method of cleansing called the prana bath. In order to do this, one pushes up the diaphragm, expelling the carbon dioxide and carbonic acid, without inhaling for some time. This is done repeatedly, according to the capacity of the lungs, but it should be practiced only under the guidance of a competent and accomplished teacher. The student first needs to be skilled in some preliminary steps of pranayama. When practiced by advanced students, the prana bath is one of the most effective cleansing techniques known and is highly regarded by the yogis dwelling in the Himalayan mountains.

Through knowledge of the respiratory system a student can gain control of the motions of the body and mind. Through the practice of pranayama he can shape his character and even change the course of his life, for the knowledge of breath is a subtle and complete way of understanding and regulating the functioning of the mind and body. A number of diseases ordinarily thought to be incurable can be helped through the practices of pranayama, for prana links the physical and mental life. When this link is broken, death takes place.

It was said by the ancient sages, "One who knows the science of breath knows everything, and he who knows prana knows the Vedas." For this very reason, "Breath is Brahman." Whatever moves or works or has life is but an expression or manifestation of prana.

To understand the science of pranayama, it is necessary to consider the nature and function of the nervous system, which coordinates the functions of all the other systems in the body. It may be subdivided into the central nervous system and the peripheral nervous system. The central nervous system consists of the brain and the spinal cord (which is an extension of the brain); the peripheral nervous system consists of the cranial nerves, spinal nerves, and most of the autonomic nervous system. The cranial nerves, spinal nerves, and the autonomic nervous system spread throughout the body, forming a network of motor and sensory nerve fibers. The motor fibers carry nerve impulses to skeletal muscles, smooth muscle in the walls of the internal organs, heart muscle, and glands; the sensory fibers carry information from the environment to the brain and spinal cord.

The autonomic nervous system regulates processes in our body that are not normally under our voluntary control—processes such as the manufacture and release of digestive secretions, the beating of the heart, and regulation of blood pressure. The autonomic nervous system is further subdivided into the sympathetic and parasympathetic nervous systems. These two systems complement one another. The sympathetic nervous system prepares the body for emergencies, and the parasympathetic nervous system supports the nurturing functions such as digestion. In some cases the two systems act in opposition on the same organ. In the heart, for example, the sympathetic nervous system speeds it up and increases the strength of contraction, and the parasympathetic nervous system slows it down.

The sympathetic nervous system consists mainly of two rows of ganglia, or nerve cell clusters, that are connected by cords made up of nerve fibers arranged vertically on either side of the spinal column. Branches from these ganglionated cords spread out to different glands and viscera in the thorax and abdomen and form plexuses or nerve centers that regulate the function of the circulatory, respiratory, digestive, urinary, endocrine, immune, and reproductive systems. In an emergency, the sympathetic nervous system speeds up the heart, releases adrenaline from the adrenal glands, and mobilizes blood sugar from the liver.

The biggest single part of the parasympathetic system is the vagus nerve, called the "wandering" nerve because it wanders down from the brain stem and controls most of the vital organs in the chest and abdomen. It contains both motor fibers that exert direct control over the functions of the internal organs and sensory fibers that carry information about the internal environment of the body back to the central nervous system. The vagus nerve slows the heartbeat, supervises digestion, and brings information to the brain regarding the oxygen and carbon dioxide content of the blood.

The science of pranayama is intimately connected with the functions of the autonomic nervous system, and its techniques are aimed at bringing these functions—normally considered involuntary—under conscious control. This can be achieved by regulating the breath and, through the breath, by controlling the motion of the lungs, the most vital step in controlling the heart rhythm and the vagus nerve. These, in turn, bring the autonomic nervous system under voluntary control. This opens the way for experiencing the higher and subtler levels of the mind. Highly accomplished yogis can also control the central nervous system so that diseases such as muscular dystrophy and Parkinson's disease can be prevented. In other words, by regulating the breath, the various vehicles responsible for conducting their respective duties in the body are regulated, good health is achieved, and the student is led to subtler levels of awareness.

The ancient manuals of yoga science describe in detail the internal structure of the human body and its functions. Even though ancient yogis did not dissect the human body, their description of the nervous system is consistent with that of modern physiology. There is, however, one major difference between the ancient descriptions and modern ones. The yogis did not refer directly to the physical details of the nervous system but to subtler counterparts of these physical details. Their texts speak of *nadis*, or subtle energy channels, and *pranas*, or vital energies, which are consistent with details of nerves and nerve impulses, respectively. In other words, physical nerves and impulses are gross manifestations of the subtler nadis and pranas, which were known to the yogis many centuries ago. Similarly, physical plexuses and gland centers are gross manifestations of the chakras, or spiritual centers, described by yogis.

Let us briefly consider the description given in ancient yogic manuals. There are several thousand nadis, of which the three main ones are *ida, pingala,* and *sushumna.* Sushumna is centrally located and passes through the *merudanda,* which corresponds to the physical spinal column. It originates at the *muladhara* chakra, corresponding to the pelvic plexus of the sympathetic system. As it passes through the merudanda it pierces the *svadhishthana* chakra, corresponding to the hypogastric plexus; the *manipura* chakra, corresponding to the solar plexus; the *anahata* chakra, corresponding to the cardiac plexus; and the *vishuddha* chakra, corresponding to the pharyngeal plexus. The sushumna then pierces the *talu,* which corresponds to the base of the skull, and divides into an anterior and a posterior portion. The anterior portion goes toward the *ajna* chakra, corresponding to the nasociliary plexus and joins the *brahma-randhra,* or cavity of Brahma, which corresponds to the ventricular cavity in the physical body. The posterior portion of the sushumna passes from behind the skull and joins the brahma-randhra. It is this posterior portion that is developed through pranayama. The realized yogi liberates his soul through the brahma-randhra.

The ida and pingala are on the left and right side, respectively, of the merudanda. They also originate in the muladhara chakra. The two nadis crisscross each other before they end at the nostrils. The ida ends in the left nostril and the pingala in the right nostril.

The yogic manuals contain detailed descriptions of the chakras, which are centers of pranic energy and which are represented as lotuses. Each chakra is associated with a certain number of petals, a certain color, a presiding deity, and so on. In the lowest center, the *muladhara* chakra, is the sleeping serpent-like fire, kundalini, which represents all the latent potential in man. It is the aim of yoga to arouse the sleeping kundalini and lead it upward through the sushumna, piercing the different chakras, to the *sahasrara* chakra, the thousand-petaled lotus at the top of the head. This represents the union of the cosmic potency, or *Shakti*, with cosmic consciousness, or *Shiva*. Through this final union the yogi achieves self-realization and liberation from all bondage. He thus merges his individual soul, Atman, with the cosmic soul, Brahman.

Pranayama practices are the means to this awakening. They aim at devitalizing the ida and pingala and allowing the prana, or vital energy, to flow through the sushumna instead. The yogi then experiences unique joy and is freed from the bondage of time.

In the human body the cosmic force or cosmic prana was subdivided by the ancients on the basis of the ten functions it performs. It is through the manifestation of these lesser pranas that all bodily functions are possible and can be co-ordinated. These are the vehicles that transport and supply the different organs of the body with cosmic energy. Of the ten pranas, five are most important: *udana, prana, samana, apana,* and *vyana.*

Udana rules the region of the body above the larynx; it governs the use of our senses. Prana rules the region between the larynx and the base of the heart and governs the vocal apparatus, the respiratory system, and the muscles engaged in breathing. Samana rules in the region between the heart and navel and governs the metabolic activity involved in digestion. Apana has its abode below the navel and governs the functions of the kidneys, colon, rectum, bladder, and genitals. Vyana pervades the whole body and governs the relaxation and contraction of all muscles, voluntary and involuntary, as well as the movement of the joints and the structures around them.

In the process of pranayama, cosmic energy in the form of prana enters the body through the vehicle of oxygen. Then during inhalation, taking the form of vyana, it reaches all the cells of the body and carries away their waste products. During exhalation the force of apana expels the waste products through the vehicle of carbon dioxide. The cessation of the movement of inhalation and exhalation and their union is called pranayama—the process by which the secret of prana and its control is understood. On attaining this union the yogi subjugates his mind and body and grasps the very core of cosmic life.

Breath is an external manifestation of the force of prana. Breath is the flywheel that regulates the entire machine of the body. Just as the flywheel of an engine controls all the other mechanisms in the machine, so control of the external breath leads to control of the gross and subtle—physical and mental—aspects of the living machine of our body.

If prana ceased to exist, thoughts would never arise, for the relationship between prana and the mind is that of the supporter and the supported. It is like the relationship between a flower and its fragrance. A comprehensive knowledge of pranayama is, therefore, of paramount importance in learning to control the mind.

The following analogy will help to make the relationship between prana and other aspects of our being more clear. In the palace of the human body there are seven chambers. The king and queen (the soul and intellect) are sitting in the innermost chamber. In the second and third chambers are the offices of the ministers (the mind), some of whom are working by day and others by night. In the fourth chamber is the office of the bodyguard of the king (the chief breath). Ten minor breaths are subordinate guards under him; they perform their duties at his command. There are three other chambers, and the king, with the help of the officers (the senses and the body), has full authority over them. Here we will discuss the role of the chief breath and its subordinates.

In this government of the human body the breath plays a vital role, for it establishes relationships between the mind and body. After a certain period of time it finally ceases waking, and when it does, the senses and the body are unable to work. With the passing away of breath, the occupants of the first and second chambers are not affected in any way, but the workers in the third to seventh chambers are paralyzed. After the breath ceases the inner organization remains intact, for the power of the king would not be diminished if the doorkeepers of the palace were to leave their jobs. So when the breath leaves the body, the link between the body and mind is broken, and the soul, intellect, and unconscious mind find another palace and begin their work anew. By the same token, if the guards in the fourth chamber of the palace run away, the king does not worry about it, for he still functions in his inner chamber.

So the wise man, who knows that even after death the soul, intellect, and mind remain quite intact, does not grieve. One who knows this reality is a true yogi. According to the second chapter of the Bhagavad Gita, the wise man is one who has experiential knowledge of prana, for without practical knowledge, reading the scriptures is mere window-shopping. (The Gita uses the word *asu* for pranas.)

Pranayama Exercises

It might surprise the reader to learn that most of the time the right and left nostrils do not work equally well. One of the nostrils is always more congested than the other even when the nasal passages are clean and unobstructed by mucus. This congestion alternates between the right and left nostrils throughout day and night. Modern physiology has only just become aware of this alternate blockage, even though anyone can test it by observing their own breathing at different times of the day. According to yoga, this phenomenon is a consequence of the alternation of the flow of subtle energy in the ida and pingala.

For meditation, it is desirable to have equal activation of these two nadis, and there are many techniques for achieving this. There are also various methods for changing the flow of breath from the active to the passive nostril. One of them is to keep the active nostril closed for some time with the fingers; the passive nostril will soon become active.

Another is to inhale through the active nostril, close it, and exhale through the passive nostril. This process is repeated several times and then reversed. Or you can inhale deeply, close both nostrils with the fingers, hold the breath for as long as is comfortable, and then release it. This should be repeated a few times, and is especially useful when you have a cold or a headache. Another method of changing the flow of breath is to make a fist, insert it into the armpit opposite the blocked nostril and apply pressure with the arm. In a few seconds the blocked nostril will open. In addition, hot and spicy food has a tendency to increase the temperature of the body and cause an increased flow in the right nostril. Exposing yourself to sudden changes of temperature also changes the breath flow.

Changing the flow of breath can cure headaches, depression, and other disorders. When the right nostril is predominant one tends to be more active and restless. Right nostril dominance is also conducive to more assertive or aggressive activities. Digestion is aided when the right nostril dominates. When the left nostril is open one is in a more passive and receptive mood. When both nostrils flow evenly one has a devotional attitude and feels a sense of harmony and joy. Having both nostrils open is ideal for meditation.

In addition to the *kriyas* described earlier, there is another simple cleansing exercise that clears the nasal passages of obstructions so that the breath can flow properly. Take a cup of lukewarm salt water and immerse the nose in it, closing one of the nostrils with one of your fingers. Inhale the water until it flows through the open nostril, into the mouth, and out. Repeat this with the other nostril. In the beginning this might cause a little discomfort, irritation, and sneezing, but that soon passes. Do this kriya each morning, and with time your nasal passages will become unobstructed and you will be free from colds, catarrh, headaches, and the like.

Let us now consider some of the simpler exercises of pranayama as well as a few more advanced ones. The higher stages of pranayama will not be discussed because they involve the use of the more challenging *bandhas,* or locks. The higher techniques must be practiced only under the guidance of a competent teacher, not on the basis of descriptions given in books, because serious physical and mental damage can result if the instructions are misunderstood or misapplied.

The following simple breathing exercises may be practiced by everyone without any danger. Through them the capacity of the lungs will be increased, and this in turn will increase resistance to the modern ills of air pollution and the like. The man who practices deep breathing will remain unaffected in situations where an ordinary man would become agitated.

Simple Deep-Breathing Exercises

After morning ablutions, stand in a calm, quiet, and airy place. Exhale through the nostrils, keeping the head, neck, and trunk erect. Try to keep the body as motionless as possible except for the motion of the abdominal and chest muscles that are involved in deep breathing. Apply the root lock by contracting the sphincter muscles of the rectum, pulling them inward and upward. Exhale through the nostrils, smoothly, without any exertion and without any sound. Having exhaled completely, do not pause but start inhaling deeply through the nostrils. Do this about ten times every morning for at least two months. Deep, rhythmic breathing, with inhalations and exhalations of equal duration has been proven beneficial for low blood pressure, insomnia, and heart attack. It strengthens the nervous system and leads to voluntary regulation of the respiratory system. This is the secret of a healthy body and a sound mind.

Another simple deep-breathing exercise is to lie on the back with the feet a comfortable distance apart and the arms alongside the body, palms up. Gently close the eyes and place the hands on the upper abdomen, between the rib cage and the navel, in order to feel the movement of the muscles. Inhale and exhale through the nostrils slowly, smoothly, and deeply. There should be no noise, jerks, or pauses in the breath. Exaggerating the normal breathing process, consciously pull in the abdominal muscles while exhaling. Aspirants who find difficulty in practicing this diaphragmatic movement may use their hands to gently push in the abdominal muscles when exhaling. When inhaling be aware of the abdominal wall pushing out. There should be a slight movement of the chest. Practice this method of deep breathing three to five minutes a day until you clearly understand the movement of the diaphragm.

Relaxation with Breathing

Relaxation with breathing has been proven useful for nervousness and other diseases. Lie down on the back with a soft pillow under the head. Cover the eyes with a piece of cloth and start exhaling and inhaling slowly and deeply, breathing diaphragmatically. First, relax the limbs physically, and then ask the mind to travel, with a feeling of relaxation, toward the toes. Do this systematically, centering on each set of muscles throughout the body and relaxing them. Start by relaxing the forehead, facial muscles, neck, shoulders, and so on, continuing down until you reach the toes. Then return to the head, relaxing each set of muscles along the way. Do not allow any other feelings to intrude during this exercise.

Relaxation should not be practiced for more than ten minutes at a time. Too much relaxation can be harmful, for if the muscles are relaxed too long the aspirant may lose control over them. What is more, one should not fall asleep during the relaxation exercises.

After relaxing for five minutes, create voluntary tension all throughout the body and try to maintain that state of tension for at least sixty seconds. Then gradually relax all parts of the body again, systematically, from head to toe. Relax, create voluntary tension, then relax again, exhaling and inhaling slowly and deeply. By concentrating on the deep and even flow of breath and thus forming the habit of deep inhalation and exhalation, it becomes possible to relax easily. In cases of fatigue, deep breathing with relaxation has been proven beneficial, but retention of the breath should be avoided. Relaxing at your office desk for five minutes is refreshing and increases the capacity for work.

Channel Purification *(Nadi Shodhanam)*

This is a breathing exercise that purifies the nadis, or subtle energy channels. It should be done at least twice a day—in the morning and in the evening. In the morning nadi shodhanam is done in the following manner:

- Sit in a calm, quiet, airy place in an easy and steady posture.
- Keep the head, neck, and trunk straight and the body still.
- Bring the right hand up to the nose. The index finger and middle finger should be folded so that the right thumb can be used to close the right nostril and the ring finger can be used to close the left nostril.

- Close the right nostril with the right thumb. Exhale completely through the left nostril. The exhalation should be slow, controlled, and free from exertion and jerks.
- At the end of the exhalation, close the left nostril with the ring finger, open the right nostril, and inhale slowly and completely. Inhalation and exhalation should be of equal duration.
- Repeat this cycle of exhaling through the left nostril and inhaling through the right nostril two more times.
- At the end of the third inhalation through the right nostril, exhale completely through that same nostril, keeping the left nostril closed with the ring finger.
- At the end of the exhalation, close the right nostril with the thumb and inhale through the left nostril.
- Repeat the cycle of exhalation through the right nostril and inhalation through the left nostril two more times. This completes the exercise.

To sum up, the exercise consists of:
- Three cycles of exhaling through the left nostril and inhaling through the right nostril followed by
- Three cycles of exhaling through the right nostril and inhaling through the left nostril.

In the evening, the exercise consists of:
- Three cycles of exhaling through the right nostril and inhaling through the left nostril followed by
- Three cycles of exhaling through the left nostril and inhaling through the right nostril.

Be careful that inhalation and exhalation are of equal duration and are slow, controlled, and free from jerks as well as any sense of exertion. With time, gradual lengthening of the duration of inhalation and exhalation should be attempted.

Ujjayi Pranayama

This pranayama should be practiced in a stable posture with the head, neck, and trunk erect. Exhale completely. Now breathe in slowly and deeply through the nostrils. The incoming air should be felt on the roof of the palate and should make a soft, continuous, sobbing sound. This is achieved by a partial closing of the glottis and is most easily done by mentally repeating *so . . . ooo* during the inbreath. The abdomen should be slightly contracted during the inhalation.

Now, without any pause, exhale the air slowly through the nostrils. The outgoing air should also be felt on the roof of the palate and should also be audible. This sound is best achieved by mentally repeating the sound *humm . . . mm* during the outbreath.

This completes one cycle of *ujjayi* pranayama. It may be repeated for about five minutes. The nasal passages are cleared through this pranayama, the nerves are soothed, and the mind is calmed.

Kapalabhati Pranayama

In literal translation *kapalabhati* means "the pranayama which makes the skull shine." It is practiced in a stable posture with the head, neck, and trunk erect and in one line. The exercise consists of a vigorous, forceful expulsion of the breath, using the diaphragm and abdominal muscles, followed by relaxation of the abdominal muscles, resulting in a spontaneous inhalation. This constitutes one cycle. Several cycles are repeated in quick succession. In the beginning you may attempt between seven and twenty-one cycles, depending on your capacity. This exercise cleans the sinuses and respiratory passages as well as stimulates the abdominal muscles and digestive organs.

Bhastrika Pranayama

Bhastra means "bellows." In this exercise the abdominal muscles move forcefully in and out like a blacksmith's bellows. In this pranayama both exhalation and inhalation are vigorous and forceful. Together they constitute one cycle, and several cycles (between seven and twenty-one) are to be repeated in quick succession. There are three variations of *bhastrika*—front bellows, side-to-side bellows, and alternate bellows. The one described above is the front bellows.

In the side-to-side bellows, the first burst of exhalation and inhalation is made with the head facing front. Now turn the head fully to the right (in the morning, but to the left in the evening) and repeat the rapid exhalation and inhalation. Now the head is turned back to the front and the exhalation/inhalation is repeated. Then to the left—exhale and inhale with a burst—and back to the front. This is one cycle. It may be repeated between seven and twenty-one times.

In the alternate bellows, the rapid exhalation/inhalation is done with one nostril at a time. The thumb of the right hand is used to close the right nostril and the rapid exhalation/inhalation takes place through the left nostril. Then the left nostril is closed with the middle or ring finger of the right hand and the rapid exhalation/inhalation takes place through the right nostril. This sequence of left nostril exhalation/inhalation and then right nostril exhalation/inhalation applies to the morning practice. It is reversed (right nostril first and then left nostril) in the evening.

The exhalation and inhalation should be vigorous and forceful, using the abdominal muscles and diaphragm, not the chest. The cycle may be repeated about twenty-one times. The benefits of bhastrika are similar to those of kapalabhati: the forceful exhalation cleans the lungs of the stale residual air which is not removed in normal breathing, the entire respiratory system is purified, and internal vigor is aroused.

Rhythmic breathing, relaxation with breathing, and both the nadi shodhanam and ujjayi pranayamas may be practiced by the beginner. Then, but only after some practice, kapalabhati and bhastrika pranayamas may be attempted.

The advanced stages of pranayama involve retention of the breath. A student can harm himself irreparably if he attempts retention without guidance and without disciplining his diet, sleep, and sex drive. Only a competent teacher can advise a practitioner when he is ready to start practicing retention. Then as the student progresses, the duration of inhalation, retention, and exhalation is extended. Finally, and only after some mastery has been achieved, retention after exhalation is also attempted.

As can be seen, pranayama is a complex and highly developed science. The fundamental exercises mentioned above can be practiced by all, but there are many more advanced techniques. The student, when convinced of the value of pranayama, is urged to seek a competent guru in order to learn the more complex practices which involve *kumbhaka* or breath retention, for through such pranayama one achieves perfection in action, speech, and thought.

CHAPTER FIVE

A Few Glimpses of Concentration

THE MIND OF the average man is scattered. He is not able to carry a single train of thought through to its desired conclusion, and his thoughts lack continuity, for his mind is largely controlled by his body and the external stimuli he receives in his daily life. In reality, however, the body is only a shadow of the mind. It is a mold prepared by the mind for its expression. It is as absurd for the body to be placed in control of the mind as it is for an employee to be in charge of his manager.

Concentration consists of bringing the scattered mind to a point of focus, for it is only through concentration that the mind can fulfill its true potential. In concentration all mental energies are brought to bear on one object or idea. The mind of the beginner rebels against the effort to concentrate, for the untrained mind finds it difficult to focus its attention exclusively on one object or idea for a sustained length of time. When the aspirant tries to slow his thinking process, for instance, thoughts resist his effort to regulate them and flit through his mind at a hectic pace. His mind

never seems free from thoughts. When one anxiety is removed, another immediately moves in, and his mind remains
distracted most of the time. Through imagination and fantasy,
too, his mind diverts him from the object of concentration.

The real glory and potential of the mind is hidden behind
a veil of instincts, impulses, emotions, moods, sentiments,
whims, and fancies. In order to understand how the mind is
so veiled, we must consider what is meant by each of these
terms. An instinct, for instance, is an involuntary prompting
to action. All humans and animals in this world have two
powerful instincts—self-preservation and reproduction.
Hunger arises from the instinct to preserve ourselves, while
lust is a manifestation of the reproductive instinct. Then
there are three kinds of impulses—impulses of thought,
speech, and action—which are intimately related to the imagination and which can be controlled by cultivating reason
and willpower.

Emotions, moods, and sentiments are interconnected but
have separate roles in the mental world. An emotion is a
combination of thought and desire, for emotions are desires
penetrated by, or merged with, thought. The basic emotions
are love and hate, and many other feelings contain elements
of these two. Reverence, for instance, is a compound of
respect and love. Of the many possible sentiments, three are
most important—the religious sentiment, the moral sentiment, and the aesthetic sentiment—and yet feelings and sentiments are ultimately illusory in nature, deceptions created
by the mind.

Moods enslave the mind. In Sanskrit the word for mood
is *bhava,* and two important bhavas are joy or exhilaration
and grief or depression. Normally the mind is continually
jumping from one bhava to another, and as a result, these

currents and crosscurrents do not allow it to consider higher realms of experience. The only truly beneficial mood is the meditative mood. In this mood, concentration comes in a spontaneous, effortless flow. Whims and fancies are present in all human beings and, in extreme cases, lead to eccentricity. Under the influence of a whim, for instance, the mind is trampled underneath, resulting in misery. Fancy is a conception of the intellectual faculty, of a lighter and less imperious cast than imagination. It helps a poet, an artist, or a dancer, but not a student of yoga when he is trying to concentrate.

Modern science tries to explain the modifications of the mind in a materialistic manner by attributing emotions, moods, and so forth, to secretions of the endocrine glands such as the thyroid, parathyroid, pineal, and thymus. According to modern science, when they are absorbed by the blood these secretions play a vital part in determining the temperament of the individual.

Yoga science, however, has a far more subtle explanation for the mind's restlessness, for it maintains that man can control his emotions by controlling his mind. Yoga science therefore focuses on knowing, analyzing, training, and controlling both the conscious and unconscious minds. For thousands of years yogis have known that the conscious part of the mind, though significant in conducting certain important duties in the external world, is only superficial. The unconscious is far more important, for in it lie the motivations behind man's activities. This fact has recently been realized by modern psychology, and research into the unconscious is finally under way. But there are many things that are not yet understood.

In yoga science an analogy is used to explain the mind: it

is like a lake disturbed by the rising waves of thoughts, or *vrittis*. The practice of concentration helps to still the waves, and when thoughts are stilled, the aspirant can see his reflection in the lake and experience his own true nature. Therefore, according to yoga science, man is not restricted to the three states of waking, dreaming, and sleeping. There is a fourth state called *turiya,* the state of the superconscious mind. To achieve it the student of yoga tries to bring his mind to a point of focus, after which he can expand it to the superconscious state. The purpose of concentration, then, is to wash off all the aspirant's impurities, to gather together the dissipated energies of his mind, and to lead the concentrated mind along one channel to the state of superconsciousness.

In everyday life we concentrate in many ways. We concentrate while inserting a thread through the eye of a needle and while driving a car through a busy street. This concentration, however, is called external, for something in the external world holds our attention. *Dharana,* or concentration, as described by Patanjali, is an internal mental process, not a muscular exercise. It takes place entirely within the field of consciousness and is directed by our will. In other words, through internal concentration the attention of the aspirant is drawn to an object and held on it through the use of willpower. Continued attention leads to concentration.

Attention is therefore preliminary to concentration. There are two kinds—voluntary and involuntary. Voluntary attention is that which is directed toward an object or idea by an effort of the will. It requires willpower, determination, and mental training. Involuntary attention, on the other hand, is spontaneous. It is a common occurrence and does not demand any practice or willpower. It is particularly noticeable among children. Concentration requires voluntary attention.

Some modern teachers advise against intense concentration, claiming this can cause tension. This is a false claim because concentration, in an advanced stage, becomes meditation. If the wandering mind is not brought home, all so-called meditational methods practiced these days will be futile. The aspirant should therefore understand that concentration is absolutely necessary, and he should not be swayed by teachings that suggest that concentration leads to tension.

There are definite techniques and processes that help in training the mind to concentrate. For instance, you should set aside a definite time each day for this purpose—morning and evening hours are best. Concentration should also be practiced under favorable circumstances. You should be alone and have determined not to be disturbed for a certain length of time. The room should be quiet, clean, and airy, without pictures or paintings on the walls. There should be no drafts in the room, the light should not be bright, and the temperature should be moderate. Concentration should not be practiced immediately after a heavy meal, as this causes discomfort and drowsiness. A regulated sexual life aids concentration. In addition, do not try to concentrate when you are physically or mentally tired, and restrict your initial sessions to about ten minutes.

Concentration is easy when the posture is steady, when the mind and body are relaxed, and when the nerves have been purified by pranayama. It is therefore advisable to practice some yoga exercises and relaxation first. Deep breathing, with regulation of the breath, stills the mind. The sitting postures recommended for meditation in an earlier chapter are suitable for concentration, or you may sit on a wooden chair with the head, neck, and trunk erect and in one line, feet planted firmly on the floor, and hands on the thighs. Do not practice concentration in *shavasana*, the supine corpse posture, as this leads to inertia and ultimately to sleep.

The mind should be untroubled and free. It should not be occupied by worldly worries and emotional problems. Yoga science includes several methods for controlling these. The first is to assume an attitude of detachment. You should gently close the eyes, withdraw the senses from the external world, and say to yourself, "Who am I? I am not the body, senses, mind, emotions, and impulses. I am the all-pervading *Atman,* or soul. How can these emotions and impulses disturb me? I am completely detached." With these positive thoughts, the impulses and emotions in the mind slowly wane.

The second method of calming the mind consists of trying to be a mere witness to your mental activity, observing silently the thought waves arising in the mind. You should not associate with passing thoughts but simply watch them flit by. No attempt should be made to use the faculties of discrimination or will, and there should be no struggle for control of the emotions and impulses, but you should note carefully the degree and duration of conflicts of attention. Repeated effort will bear fruit. The initial attempts may be frustrating; only patience and perseverance will lead to success. However, if the conflicts are insurmountable, the practice should be halted and continued at a more suitable time, for there should be no sense of effort involved in any method of concentration. Effort leads to tension, and tension upsets the nervous system and results in serious discomfort.

There are various types of concentration—gross, subtle, outer, inner, objective, subjective, and infinite, depending on the object of concentration. The choice of the object is an important consideration for if it is pleasant, this makes the task easier.

In the beginning one should concentrate on external objects, such as a point, a candle flame that does not flicker, a photograph of Christ, Krishna, Buddha, or the guru. One could also choose a blue, red, or yellow flower, or use a mirror and gaze at the midspace between the eyebrows in the reflection. The gaze should be steady, but there should be no strain in the eyes. It should be held for only a minute or two at a time, but this may be repeated two or three times. The early sessions should not last very long. Intensity of concentration is more important than duration of practice. After a while the time span should slowly be increased.

The nasal gaze and frontal gaze are also effective methods for developing concentration. In the nasal gaze, the eyes are gently focused on the tip of the nose, whereas in the frontal gaze, the space between the eyebrows is the point of concentration. There should be no violent or forceful effort involved in this practice, and the duration of concentration should gradually be increased from half a minute, or one minute, to half an hour. The method of concentration chosen should be based on one's temperament, but once the method has been chosen, the aspirant should practice it faithfully for at least three months. Only then will he begin to see results.

In the types of concentration mentioned so far the eyes are open and focused on an external object. This is called *trataka.* We now come to methods of concentration in which the eyes are closed. Here, three means are used:

Concentration on a word or sound, such as the eternal word *Om,* creates vibrations and forms a mental image. When this subtle form is established in the mind, the mind becomes steady.

Concentration on exhalation and inhalation while repeating a mantra, or eternal word, brings home wandering thoughts.

Concentration on a mental image also makes the mind steady. In the beginning the mental image chosen should be that of a concrete, simple object, such as a small illuminated circle or a soothing light, and efforts should be made to hold the mental image for as long as possible. Abstract or complicated objects or ideas should not be attempted in the beginning. Other suitable images are the written form of *Om,* the form of Christ, Krishna, Buddha, or the guru.

When the eternal word or spiritual object is chosen by the guru, the aspirant may have psychic experiences—such as hearing celestial sounds, smelling exquisite fragrances, or knowing the future—when these techniques of concentration are used. All these experiences are bright milestones on the path of progress. They help inspire the aspirant, but he should not dwell on them or consider them an end in themselves. They are only by-products of concentration. The real goal is ultimate truth and realization.

There are more advanced methods of concentration. In one method the *ajna* chakra, located between the eyebrows, is chosen as the object of concentration. This is the seat of the mind in the waking state and is an important and sensitive center. Light is seen here during concentration. This particular region of concentration is suitable for making the mind inwardly directed, one-pointed, and steady. Powers of clairvoyance also result from concentration at this spot, which in Sanskrit is termed *divya-chakshu,* or the divine eye. Concentration on the *anahata* chakra, the heart center, is another method which leads to great joy, for the anahata chakra is the seat of all emotions and feelings. It is the yogic heart, between the two breasts, not the heart of flesh. Yogis avoid concentration on the lower plexuses.

It is believed that concentrating on the ajna chakra brings all the other chakras under its command, and those who are intellectual are often advised to concentrate here. However, those who are emotional and sensitive are advised to concentrate instead on the anahata chakra, the lotus of the heart. Concentration on either chakra stills the mind. Prolonged concentration leads to meditation and eventually to the awakening of the kundalini and its passage through the *sushumna.* The aspirant then experiences limitless bliss and realizes the ultimate reality. The awakening of the kundalini is possible, however, only with the help of a competent guru.

There are many other methods of concentration mentioned in the Upanishads and yogic manuals, but they are often not elaborated upon and are fully revealed only to initiates by competent gurus. Some of these are *bindu-bhedana, madhu-vidya,* and *shakti-chalana.* Bindu means "a point or dot," and in *bindu-bhedana* the bindu is visualized at the ajna chakra as a tiny transparent pearl until the vision is clear. Then the pearl-like bindu is moved to the sahasrara chakra. In this practice the bindu is regarded as the essence of the mind, and the mind is enriched by direct contact with the resulting superconscious state.

Another advanced method prescribes concentration on the solar breath in the right nostril (associated with thought) as being wedded to the lunar breath in the left nostril (associated with feeling). *Jnana,* or knowledge, is the child born of this union. It is also called *sushumna,* or the joyous mind.

Yogic methods for developing concentration are scientific and exact, and in all of them attention and willful withdrawal of attention are brought under conscious control. Then, in the second stage of concentration, voluntary and involuntary movements of the mind are also brought under conscious control. This type of concentration is quite unlike that which is taught to us by parents and teachers. The methods used in schools and universities are one-sided, for they relate to the conscious mind alone. We are taught how to take off, so to speak, but no one teaches us how to land. The process of thinking without a definite direction and goal dissipates the energy of the mind, and the thinker does not know how to come back to where he started. Such one-sided teaching can be damaging and even dangerous.

Therefore, concentration is an aspirant's foremost duty. According to Adi Shankara, the most famous exponent of Advaita Vedanta philosophy, the aspirant's duty consists of two things: controlling the senses and concentrating the mind. Until the thoughts of the aspirant are completely controlled, he should strive ceaselessly, concentrating his mind on one truth at a time.

Concentration is in opposition to sensual desires. When the mind becomes desireless, free from dwelling on sense objects and their enjoyment, *dhyana,* or meditation (the state referred to as *nididhyasana* by the Vedantins) is achieved. Concentration is therefore the master key that opens the gates of meditation, for prolonged concentration results in meditation. In fact, it is difficult to discern the dividing line between the two.

Without concentration the energy of the mind is dissipated in vague thoughts, worries, and fantasies. A man of ordinary intellect, with highly developed concentration, is more creative than a highly intelligent man with poor concentration. Through concentration a direct link with the cosmic mind is established so that the mind can attend to several things simultaneously. Concentration is no substitute for labor or action, but it does assist the individual in gaining unique experiences and truths hidden in the deeper recesses of the mind.

Patanjali gave elaborate treatment to the science of concentration, for he realized its utility in calming an agitated mind. Modern scientists now concur with this view and are convinced that only through concentration is it possible to gather together scattered forces and emotions, and resolve conflicts. With steady practice the nervous system and the mind are relaxed, and the mind then becomes steady, one-pointed, and free from the shackles of desire. The aspirant is thus led, through concentration, to the superconscious state where he experiences the bliss divine.

· CHAPTER SIX ·

Mind and Its Analysis

ACCORDING TO YOGA SCIENCE the brain gets rest during sleep, but the mind does not. However, the yogi who has controlled his mind derives the joy of rest from meditation, and therefore needs little sleep. It is through the mind that the all-pervading *Brahman,* or universal spirit, manifests itself. In *samadhi,* which according to raja yoga is the final abode of bliss, the mind goes to its original seat, where its presiding deity resides.

The origin of the mind is *atma-shakti,* the capacity of the Self; the seat of the mind is the *brahma-randhra,* the cavity of the brain. In Sanskrit the cosmic mind is called *hiranya-garbha,* the golden womb; *karya-brahman,* causal consciousness; and *sambhuti,* consciousness consisting of all minds. According to the Bhagavad Gita the mind is one of the *ashta-prakritis,* or eight primary elements, namely earth, water, fire, air, space, lower mind, intellect, and ego. In the philosophy of raja yoga and Sankhya philosophy, the term *mahat* denotes the cosmic or universal mind, the first principle manifested out of the unmanifested one, Brahman. Just as a wheel rests on its spokes, and the spokes rest on an axle, so does our mind rest on the cosmic mind, and the cosmic mind rests on Brahman.

If we think of the cosmic mind as the source of all individual minds, and if we think of it as represented by energy, then all the creatures of the world would be like small illumined bulbs. Just as electricity is generated in a powerhouse and flows into bulbs, so power from the cosmic mind flows into individual minds, filling them with the illumination of consciousness. The cosmic mind is subtle and is in close contact with other minds. In other words, as our mind evolves, we enter into a conscious relationship with other minds. Numerous minds are linked in this way, and this network forms part of *mahat*, the cosmic mind. This is called the *vibhu* theory of raja yoga.

From mahat comes *ahankara*, or ego, and from the *sattvic* ahankara, or pure tranquil ego, comes *manas*, the lower mind. From the *rajasic* ahankara, or active ego, come the *indriyas*, the faculties of perception and action; from the *tamasic* ahankara, or inert ego, come the *tanmatras*, the subtle elements, from which arise the gross elements that form this universe. The mind, as understood by yoga psychology, is fourfold. Together, the four aspects of mind constitute *antahkarana*, the inner instrument, which is made up of *manas*, the lower mind; *buddhi*, the intellect or faculty of discrimination; *ahankara*, the ego; and *chitta*, the mind-stuff.

Manas, the lower mind, is the link between the senses of perception (sight, sound, smell, taste, touch), the senses of action (grasping, speaking, locomoting, excreting, procreating), and the buddhi, the discriminative faculty. It also transmits the commands of buddhi to the active senses. Buddhi is the correlate of mahat, the cosmic intelligence, on the plane of the individual. It is both the will and the faculty of discrimination combined. Buddhi sorts out sensory input, and when it arrives at a decision, ahankara steps in and expresses that decision as a thought, such as "I like this ice cream" or "I wonder who he is?" and so on. All of this mental activity takes place in the chitta, the canvas on which one's mental activities are painted, which also retains the impressions of these activities in the bed of memory. The unconscious is, therefore, a part of chitta.

Although it is made up of these four aspects, the mind is actually one unit. It is like a tree. The seed is the idea of "I" arising from the ego; the sprout springing up from this seed is buddhi; and the branches of the tree are the *sankalpas,* or thoughts and reflections. The mind extends through past, present, and future, having various functions but remaining one. To give an analogy, a person may be a professor at a college, a husband to his wife, a father to his children, and so on. But he is the same person even though he fulfills many functions. So it is with the mind. When it thinks and doubts, it is manas; when it wills and discriminates, it is buddhi; when it arrogates, it is ahankara; when it stores thoughts of the past and the present, it is chitta. One beautiful quality of the mind is that when any one of its aspects functions, all the others begin to function too. Another characteristic of the mind is that it always attaches itself to something objective. It cannot stand by itself and function independently. It is always dependent, in one way or another, on a thought form, symbol, idea, or image.

There are three bodies which envelop the *Atman,* or Self, and which shroud its true glory. The innermost is the *karana sharira,* or seed body. It is with this body that a yogi passes on from one physical body to another. It is from this body that the other two bodies arise, hence the name "seed," or causal body. The next is the *sukshma sharira,* or subtle body, consisting of seventeen *tattvas,* or primary substances. These are: the ten *indriyas* (the five senses of perception—the faculties of sight, hearing, taste, smell, and touch, as well as the five active faculties consisting of speech, the capacity to hold and grasp, the ability to move, to procreate, and to excrete, as mentioned earlier); the five *tanmatras,* or subtle elements, out of which sight, sound, smell, taste, and touch are composed within the mind; the manas, or lower mind; and the buddhi, or discriminative faculty. The outermost body is the *sthula sharira,* or physical body, which is linked to the total mind through the *pranas.* At death the physical body dies and the pranas dissipate, while the causal body travels to different realms and is subsequently linked with another physical body. Death is the habit of the physical body, but the Atman, or center of consciousness, is ever existent. When, through meditation, the stage of samadhi, or self-realization, is attained, the causal body also drops off, and the Atman merges in Brahman—the drop of water has become one with the mighty ocean.

The soul is the only source of intelligence, and it shines by its own light; the mind and senses derive their activity from it. The soul is the subject, and the mind is its object. According to the Vedas, the most ancient *rishi,* or seer, is the soul who sees through the mind. The ego, then, is not conscious in and of itself because it does not shine by its own light, but reflects the light of consciousness shining from the innermost Self, just as the moon has no inherent light of its own, but reflects the light of the sun.

Just as the physical body is composed of solid, liquid, and gaseous matter, so is the mind or subtle body made up of various subtle vibrations. Just as physical bodies vary from person to person, so also do the subtle bodies of different people. It is also true that every man has a mental world of his own, and there are vast differences between any two minds, for the mind is both single and minute as an atom *(anu)* and simultaneously all-pervading *(vibhu)*. The beauty of the cosmic mind is found in its variegated nature.

In Sanskrit we refer to *tejas,* the brilliance that emanates from the mind; for the developed minds of yogis have an effulgent aura which can affect in a beneficial manner those who are prepared to come under its influence. That is how telepathy is established between two lovers, or between a yogi and his disciples. That is how a strong mind influences a weak mind. Some people develop a more sensitive and organized thought force than others, and one who has purified his mind becomes a center of this force. That is why weaker minds are unconsciously drawn to purified minds—because they derive peace, power, strength, and joy from the greater force emanating from that mind. For instance, aspirants are benefited more when they are in the presence of their master. Even though the guru may not speak a word, the student can feel a thrilling sensation and derive new inspiration from his mere presence. For one who has an undeveloped mind it is necessary to surrender to a virtuous and purified mind, for unless one surrenders, the higher mind takes some time to influence the lower mind. Fortunate are those who have such opportunities.

The mind is a collection of thoughts and habits. It is a huge heap of desires gathered from contact with the different forces of the world, for it is the habit of the mind to collect feelings aroused by worldly disturbances. The mind gathers impressions from ever-changing sources and is a storehouse of new and old desires. This does not interfere with its mental operations, for some of the old desires depart as new arrivals make their abode in the subtle mind, and the mental harmony of thought, feeling, and desire is sustained. The mind changes its color and shade every minute, but beliefs and the powers of judgment and discrimination change only after several years, because the mind evolves through its experiences slowly.

Who teaches the mind? Its own experiences. Man corrects his views with the help of new experience and knowledge. He also builds his conscience in this way, for conscience consists of one's own convictions arrived at either instinctively or by reasoning. The conscience of a yogi and the conscience of an ordinary man, for instance, are entirely different, for the conscience of a yogi is like a clean mirror reflecting his own inner light.

Sensation, thought, and volition are the threefold functions of the mind, and it has three states—active, passive, and neutral. It always rejects monotony. Association, continuity, and relativity are the three principal laws of the mind. Broadly speaking, there are three aspects of the mind—the conscious or objective mind, the unconscious or subjective mind, and the superconscious mind.

The mind, intellect, and understanding are in the subtle body, but they operate through the physical brain. We will clarify this statement by returning to the simile of the king and his kingdom. Though a king has complete command over his kingdom and has palaces in different places, he has his most splendid palace in the capital. So it is with the mind. Though the mind has all-pervading power in the body, according to the experience of yogis it has three different residences during the three states of waking, dreaming, and deep sleep. In the waking state the seat of the mind is the *ajna* chakra, which is situated in the space between the eyebrows. This is its most splendid palace. Just notice what you do in deep thought. You place a finger on your chin, turn your neck to the right, gaze toward the space between your eyebrows, and begin to ponder the problem at hand. This shows that during the waking period the mind resides in the ajna chakra.

The Atman, the source of the mind, is pure consciousness, and the mind is illumined by its brilliance. Just as an iron rod in a fire borrows heat and light, so the mind, being an instrument only and nonconscious, appears self-aware by borrowing light from its source, the Atman.

The mind can do only one thing at a time, for it is finite. (In Sanskrit the mind is sometimes called *paricchinna*, meaning "limited.") It is ever fluctuating, full of impulses, habits, and emotions. It is the instrument through which sensations and thoughts arise, but it must be under the control of someone. For instance, if one controls his mind he will know that the thinker is different from the thought. During deep sleep the functioning of the mind is quieted, so the mind is not the source of life and light. It cannot be taken for the pure Self, for it is full of impurities. It becomes excited during anger, trembles in fear, and shrinks in shock. So the mind is not the Atman. The human soul is also not the director of the mind because we see that ordinary men cannot control their mind. There is someone else in control of the mind, called *manaspati* in Sanskrit, "lord of the mind," and if one dives deep into the lake of his thinking, he will find that someone silently witnessing the lake and its various waves. But as long as the ripples of the mind are not calmed, the Atman, or true Self within, cannot be seen.

Ordinarily, we make a mistake in defining the word *knowledge*, not realizing it has four distinct sources: instinct, reason, intuition, and superintuition. An animal is not able to know itself because it has only physical consciousness. All of its activities are governed by instinct. In a way, however, the work done by them through instinct is more perfect than that of humans. For instance, if one notices the excellent work done by the birds in building their beautiful nests, he will marvel at the power of instinct.

Next comes reason. Reason is higher than instinct and is found only in human beings. It is developed by strengthening the faculty of discrimination. The more it is sharpened, the more the intellect gains the power of penetration. Intellect can travel to higher realms if it is purified, trained, and cultivated, and through such an intellect come spiritual flashes. For instance, after collecting facts, and reasoning from cause to effect as well as from proposition to proof, the intellect can make judgments and take one safely to the gate of intuition.

Intuition is a spiritual experience. The supersensory knowledge of intuition is gained through the functioning of the subtle body. It is a higher source of knowledge than intellect, for in intuition there is no reasoning. It is called *divya-drishti*, or divine sight, for spiritual inspiration, insight, and revelation from the inner world come through intuition and not through intellect. Beyond intuition is the realization of the Self, and this transcends even the subtle body. This is the highest knowledge of reality.

The physical body is an instrument by which the mind gains experience from the objects of the world through the five organs of perception. All the senses are used as instruments for gaining experience and knowledge, for the mind is the life-instrument of this body and moves all the limbs according to the data it receives through the sense organs. Just as a garden cannot exist without water, so the body cannot survive without mental actions, which the mind performs with great speed. The body is the projection of the mind, and the mind is the subtle form of the body; the mind contemplating the body becomes the body itself, and is then afflicted by it.

Before anything happens in this outer world of ours, something has already happened in the inner world. Before any action is done, it is done by the mind in its mental workshop. Every cell in this body receives an impulse from every thought that enters the mind. When the mind is turned to a particular thought and ponders it for some time, a definite vibration is started, and this vibration repeats itself until it eventually becomes a habit, because the body follows the mind and imitates it.

The mind is the subtle counterpart of the physical body, and the physical body is the manifestation of the mind, so when the mind becomes tense, the body becomes tense, and when the mind is relaxed, the body is also relaxed. States of mind are noticeably reflected on the face, for instance. Just as the tongue is the index of the stomach, so the face is the index of the mind. One may foolishly think that he can hide his thoughts, but thoughts, emotions, and sentiments produce quite noticeable expressions on the face.

There is a mutual relationship between the mind and body. The two are intimately connected. The mind acts upon the body, and the body reacts upon the mind. A pure, healthy mind results in a healthy body because thoughts are the primary cause of all the ills of life. Whatever one holds in one's mind will produce an effect in the physical body.

Violent fits of temper, for instance, seriously damage the brain cells, inject poisonous chemicals into the blood, produce shocks in the nervous system that suppress secretions of gastric juice, bile, and other secretions in the alimentary canal, and drain away energy and vitality, thus inducing premature old age and death. But the pains and sufferings of the physical body are actually secondary to the diseases of the mind.

On the other hand, if unwanted and undesirable thoughts are controlled, all diseases will vanish. Therefore the aspirant should keep a strict watch on incoming and outgoing thoughts, emotions, and feelings, and should accept or reject them according to their effects and consequences. One is able to do this more easily if the mental atmosphere has been favorably prepared through the *yamas* and *niyamas*. With the right mental attitude, the posture being steady and the breathing deep and even, and the senses being withdrawn from the distractions outside, then the mind's outward activity is checked and it starts traveling inward. Awareness of the mind's activities and control of these activities through voluntary attention leads to a state of concentration. The mind is now one-pointed, in a state of focus. That which was diffuse is now capable of penetrating the levels of the conscious and unconscious into the expanse of the superconscious. The aspirant is now in the state of meditation.

· CHAPTER SEVEN ·

What Is Meditation?

MEDITATION IS NOT properly understood in the Western world. Some people think of it as concentration, others understand it to be silent prayer. In the *Encyclopedia Britannica,* for instance, the word *meditation* has been explained as concentration, but the word *concentration* has not been explained further. Modern dictionaries define meditation variously as follows: (1) sustained reflection; the turning or revolving of any subject in the mind; close or continued thought; (2) a private devotional act consisting of deliberate reflection upon some spiritual truth or mystery, accompanied by mental prayer and resolutions as to future conduct; (3) a private religious or devotional exercise consisting of a continuous application of the mind to the consideration of some religious or moral truth, or the like, in order to promote holiness or love of God.

None of these definitions explains the word *meditation* accurately. It is properly defined by the Sankhya school of philosophy as *dhyanam nirvishayam manah,* which may be translated into English as "the liberation of the mind from all disturbing and distracting emotions, thoughts, and desires."

Typically, our mind is restless and confused. Our attention flits from one thought to another. Through the course of a single day we may experience many unpleasant emotions, such as anxiety, depression, disappointment, anger, and frustration, and we are pulled here and there by our many desires. We are easily distracted and find it difficult to find a center of equilibrium, and there is scarcely a chance to find rest and renewal.

Few people know that meditation is a practice which, from the very beginning, helps us to find stability and calmness. We become freed from restless desires, from the disturbing thoughts which normally come before our mind, and from our emotional reactions. As we progress in the practice of meditation, we find that disturbances are gradually replaced by an ever-increasing sense of peace and happiness. Our mental and emotional environment becomes purified, and we experience a sense of inner refreshment and joy.

Through meditation an aspirant's cognition, emotion, and volition become unified, and his latent powers are awakened. Only through such a total integration of the mind is it possible to develop a dynamic personality. All the glorious deeds in human history have been achieved by men of concentrated willpower. On the other hand, Western psychologists, psychiatrists, and physiologists have begun to realize that the human mind is the originator of conflicting urges and emotions as well, and that many diseases have their origin in the unconscious. What they do not yet know is that these conflicts in the mind can be resolved through meditation.

Meditation begins with concentration, for through concentration the mind becomes steady and one-pointed. When concentration leads to the uninterrupted flow of the mind toward one object, this becomes meditation. The mind is then expanded to the higher realms of the superconscious state. Thus, meditation is the process through which the mind is first made one-pointed and then expanded to the state of enlightenment. It involves a subtle yet definite conscious effort.

The science of meditation was developed systematically in ancient India during the Upanishadic period. It was elaborated upon later by the seer Patanjali, and the techniques spread far and wide. For example, a school of meditation was established by Indian monks in Egypt around the third or fourth century A.D. and in China around 525 A.D. Later, the teachings traveled to Japan. In fact, the word *Zen* is derived from the Sanskrit word *dhyana,* which means "meditation." In the Christian tradition a school of meditation was established by Saint Anthony, and the methods of meditation were known to great souls such as Saint Francis and others, but due to fear that its practitioners would become the object of religious persecution, the art of meditation remained hidden in the hearts of a few wise saints.

Through the centuries meditation has developed into a highly evolved and systematic science for expanding consciousness, for in yoga blind faith is always discouraged. Certain practices are described, as are the results that can be achieved through their use, and the aspirant is expected to convince himself of their validity experientially. With this empirical approach, therefore, a person's firsthand experience of a state of consciousness is the proof of its existence. No other proof can be given; indeed, no other proof is necessary.

In his *Yoga Sutra,* Patanjali mentions certain powers a yogi may acquire through concentration and meditation. For example, through sustained and prolonged concentration on the hollow of the throat a yogi can transcend hunger and thirst. Such a claim can be verified only by practicing the concentration method specified.

So yoga is a voyage of discovery, in which one explores his inner self, aided by the directions given to him by the illumined yogis who have trodden the same paths and reached the final goal. Such directions, both general and specific, are given in the *Yoga Sutra* and in other ancient manuals. However, if we are treading a specific path, each one of us must also seek the aid of a guru, a spiritual teacher and guide, for a guru, having realized these truths experientially, holds the key to ultimate truth.

Methods of Meditation

Let us now consider the methods of meditation. Before the aspirant can attain a state of meditation he should have practiced six preliminary steps, and every time he meditates, he should go through them in order to reach a meditative state.

The first step is to establish the right mental atmosphere. Being mindful of the *yamas* and *niyamas,* the ten principles of living graciously in the world and expanding self-awareness, helps the student in composing his mind and establishing harmony within himself. For instance, if he is in an angry mood he tries to wash away his anger by reminding himself of the principle of *ahimsa,* or nonharming. Paying mental homage to the guru, and to the long line of sages through whom he has received the teaching, also helps in establishing a favorable mental background for meditation.

Before the student assumes the meditative posture it is helpful to go through some relaxation exercises practiced in *shavasana*, the corpse posture. This is the second step. Relaxation can be achieved on three levels: relaxation of the nervous system, the internal organs, and the mind. Relaxation exercises range from the elementary to the advanced ones that aim at withdrawing into the subtle body. Relaxation, with deep breathing, proceeds systematically from head to toe, and back upward.

Relaxation and concentration are intertwined. It is impossible for a tense person to concentrate, for tension indicates restlessness and disturbance in both the physical body and the mind. Systematic relaxation, on the other hand, leads the mind toward concentration as it focuses on the various parts of the body, one by one. Each muscle and joint is relaxed completely through this kind of concentration, which has been used to cure hypertension, tension headaches, and the like. Physical relaxation also leads to calmness of the mind. Alpha brain waves predominate in the relaxed state, and in the more advanced relaxation exercises, theta waves (which are indicative of concentration and creativity) predominate.

Having tried to relax the body, nerves, and mind, the aspirant then goes to the third step by assuming a meditative posture that is steady and comfortable and that ensures that the head, neck, and trunk are erect and in one straight line. The body should be made absolutely motionless, thus bringing the *karmendriyas*, or active senses, under control. The practitioner will find that, as time goes by, merely sitting motionless in a meditative posture will induce a feeling of peace and joy.

The fourth step is to practice some pranayama exercises while sitting in a meditative posture. These involve control of the breath and vital energy, and they purify the body and nervous system. Exercises such as *kapalabhati* and *bhastrika* empty the stale air from the lungs, increase the oxygen supply to the body, make the mind alert and free from drowsiness, and will, in time, clear up the nasal and respiratory passages. Breathing becomes more deep and even. *Nadi shodhanam* strengthens the nervous system, purifies the *nadis,* or subtle energy channels, and clears the mind. Thus the right and left breaths are equalized, and breathing becomes deeper and more gentle. These breathing exercises eventually lead to the deeper stages of sense withdrawal and concentration.

The fifth step is *pratyahara,* control of the *jnanendriyas,* or senses of perception. Here, the practitioner becomes aware of the space immediately around him, withdraws his awareness from all other times, and experiences the present moment more completely. He tries to be "here and now," and then makes a *sankalpa,* or resolution, by mentally affirming, "I am not the body, I am not the senses—they are my instruments. I am not the mind. The mind is my subtler instrument. I am the *Atman,* the infinite." Every time the mind tries to wander outward, the practitioner should gently draw it back inward.

This leads to the last step. Here, the aspirant then tries to make his mind one-pointed through voluntary attention and concentration. He now becomes aware of his breath and synchronizes it with a mantra, such as so hum, "I am That." *So . . . ooo* is synchronized with the inbreath and *hum . . . mm* with the outbreath. The practitioner concentrates on the breath, beginning in the nostrils and proceeding inward along the energy channels in the nose-bridge, eyebrow center, and spine.

Concentration makes the mind one-pointed, and pro-longed concentration enables one to go further, piercing the conscious and unconscious and expanding the mind to the level of the superconscious. Not all methods of concentration will lead to the superconscious, however. Only the methods prescribed by the guru, based on his evaluation of the aspirant's capacity and needs, will lead to the superconscious state. The practitioner needs the guidance and grace of the guru.

Guru and Mantra

The first stage of guidance is initiation into a specific mantra. The aspirant may be advised to concentrate on a particular sound, light, or chakra along with the mantra. Through initiation into a chakra, or center of integration, the spiritual energy of that center can be awakened, and the blocked channels of subtle energy can be opened. This cannot be accomplished by the aspirant on his own; it is possible only through the initiatory power of a guru, who is a channel for the power which flows down a long line of gurus, dating back many thousands of years. There are more advanced stages of initiation beyond this, one following the other, until the aspirant reaches full realization of his divine nature through the grace of the guru.

There are two Sanskrit words, *dhyana* and *nididhyasana,* both of which are sometimes translated as "meditation." There is a difference, however. *Nididhyasana* is more correctly translated as "reflection or contemplation." It is the method used in the monastic tradition of Vedanta, one of the seven schools of Indian philosophy. In this practice a senior monk assigns a novice a certain truth to reflect upon.

The truth is usually contained in a brief sentence such as "Thou art That" or "I am Brahman." Starting with linguistic analysis and discursive thought, the novice continues to reflect on the truth until the intellect is transcended. The entire energy of thought is thus absorbed into the inner personality, and the novice begins to have a direct personal experience of the inner, intuitive aspect of the truth on which he is reflecting.

Dhyana, or meditation, however, is a different process. Here a conscious, voluntary attempt is made to still the activity of the conscious mind. Through withdrawal of the senses and concentration, one-pointedness of mind is achieved, and then, like the continuous flow of oil from one vessel to another, concentration flows into meditation. This uninterrupted flow of attention leads to timelessness, and intuitive knowledge dawns.

The transition from one-pointedness of the conscious mind to expansion into the superconscious is possible, however, only through the guru's grace. Without grace the aspirant who stills the conscious mind becomes aware only of the murky depths of the unconscious. This is a maze of diverse impressions, and one can lose himself in it so completely that he cannot transcend the unconscious to attain the superconscious state. The occult sciences are based on this experience of the dark shadows of the unconscious, a state which represents a fall from the conscious to the unconscious rather than an ascent from the conscious into the purity of the superconscious.

Let us consider some of the techniques which, when prescribed by a guru, lead to the superconscious experience. But remember that even though they may be mentioned in detail in books, they do not take the aspirant very far unless they are prescribed by a competent teacher. In Patanjali's *Yoga Sutra* various methods of meditation are outlined, which are to be used according to the capacity and ability of the aspirant. One such method is mantra yoga. The word *mantra* means "that which liberates the mind from all grief and sorrow." It is a secret teaching imparted by the guru to his disciple when the latter is initiated into the yoga tradition, and consists of one or more words, chosen by the guru, specifically for leading a particular aspirant to the final truth. It is considered to be sacred. Not every word can be a mantra, and a mantra is not composed by the guru. Mantras have been handed down to him through his tradition, having been revealed to great yogis and seers while they were in a superconscious state. The science of mantra is exact, and few people know or understand its true significance. But once initiated, the disciple repeats and meditates upon the mantra throughout his life, and gradually it will lead him to the state of *samadhi*.

Japa is the act of continually repeating the mantra, which has to become an essential part of the aspirant's life. Starting with mere repetition of the mantra, the disciple is led spontaneously to meditation upon its meaning and then to the realization of the truth it contains. The mantra also works on the level of the unconscious mind, controlling moods and combating and overcoming undesirable emotional states, such as anger, greed, lust, sloth, and the like. In addition, it purifies his mind, making him capable of the degree of concentration necessary for his subsequent evolution into superconsciousness. The practice of japa is found in most religions of the world and is considered to be a form of prayer by those who employ it.

In the scriptures it is said that when the disciple is ready, the guru appears. He need not be a human being, however. In the Hindu scriptures there are many instances of aspirants having been initiated in their dreams by great saints, and the mantras received in such dream experiences are considered to be as sacred as those received in the waking state from a human guru. Concentration upon such a dream experience is also one of the methods of meditation, but the aspirant should be careful not to believe that all dreams are of divine origin. The truly inspired dream experience brings with it a sense of joyous revelation and is easily distinguished from other dreams.

Meditation upon the Self

The ultimate goal of meditation is to experience the Self, pure consciousness. The experience of one's innermost Self is a state of transcendent knowledge and bliss. It is that state beyond time, space, and causation which has been variously called samadhi, *nirvana,* and cosmic consciousness. When the mind is completely centered for an extended period of time, when it is not distracted by various thoughts or external objects, we become aware of the essence of our being, the Atman. Ordinarily awareness is not refined enough to perceive the Self. The mind is preoccupied with more gross perceptions and thoughts, but the practice of concentration and meditation gradually sharpens our perception of the inner workings of the real Self, which is hidden within.

The Atman is covered by three sheaths. The outermost is the physical sheath, composed of gross matter. Beneath this is the subtle sheath, composed of subtler counterparts of gross matter. The innermost sheath is the causal body, which has been fashioned out of our actions by the law of karma. In normal waking consciousness all three sheaths intervene between the aspirant and Atman, but during the dream state the physical sheath is removed, and in the state of dreamless sleep only the causal sheath shrouds the Atman. We are therefore closest to the Atman in the state of dreamless sleep, but no memory of the experience remains when we wake up, for this sheath is difficult to penetrate. This is why one cannot achieve a realization of the Atman merely through dreamless sleep. One of the methods of meditation consists of trying to bring back into the waking state the experience of the state of dreamless sleep. This involves dwelling upon and trying to intensify the sense of peace that lingers into the waking state after experiencing dreamless sleep.

In the Upanishads it is stated that the Atman dwells within the lotus of the heart. This doesn't refer to the heart of flesh, but to the anahata chakra. In the *Katha Upanishad* the Atman is described as a smokeless, pure, illumined flame the size of the thumb in the shrine of the heart. In their deeper states of meditation yogis experience the lotus of the heart, and bathed in its inner light, they experience divine bliss. One of the more advanced methods of meditation consists of meditating on the lotus of the heart after making the mind steady through concentration. Then, withdrawing from the objects of the senses, the aspirant enters this shrine of Atman and, meditating there, transcends the body and experiences higher knowledge.

When a practitioner first begins to concentrate, he is faced with all sorts of distractions. Many aspirants grow discouraged, feeling that they were calmer before they started the practice. This feeling is a result of experiencing disturbances that have always existed, but which were previously outside of the aspirant's awareness. It is like seeing for the first time all the dust that has been swept under the carpet. This stage is transitory. If the aspirant perseveres he will go beyond it and achieve the necessary one-pointedness of mind.

In the practice of concentration the aspirant is concerned with the external aspects of objects. Then concentration gives way to meditation in which he perceives the innermost nature of the object of concentration. Meditation finally leads to samadhi, in which the aspirant achieves oneness with the object of concentration.

In the lower stages of samadhi, though perfect concentration has been achieved, the seeds of desire and attachment still remain in a latent state. Liberation from all bondage comes only in the higher stages of samadhi when these seeds no longer exist. Then the mind is open to receive direct superconscious knowledge, which is beyond all perception by the senses and all comprehension by the intellect.

There are three processes that take place in the mind during meditation: contemplation, filling, and identification. The aspirant should remember these three word-images before starting his meditation. Contemplate Atman; fill the mind with Atman; then you will become identified with Atman. As you think, so you become. Think you are Atman, and Atman you will become.

Meditation Through Self-Surrender

There is one method of yoga in which neither postures nor techniques of concentration and meditation are involved. This is self-surrender, the highest of all the yogas. The twentieth-century sage Sri Aurobindo and his followers call self-surrender "Integral Yoga." It is described by Lord Krishna in the eighteenth chapter of the Bhagavad Gita. According to this method one should surrender the body, mind, intellect, and ego entirely to the ultimate reality in order to bring down into one's daily life the peace, purity, truth, consciousness, and bliss of the supreme Self.

The qualities of peace and purity are often misunderstood. When we talk of peace, it is not the peace of the tomb to which we refer. Rather, it is a peace which permeates all aspects of life. It fuses our mind, actions, and speech, keeping us balanced and harmonized. It illuminates our life. Its source is not found in temples, churches, or mosques, nor is it found in the rigidity of rituals and ceremonies or in the external worship of idols. It resides in the human soul as a manifestation of divine love. Purity, also, is often misunderstood. Purity means to accept no influence other than the influence of the divine. Mere external washing is meant to keep the body pure, but mental purity leads from intellect to intuition.

Two other qualities of action characterize the life of the aspirant whose method is self-surrender: faithfulness and sincerity. Faithfulness is to admit and to manifest no movement other than that which is prompted and guided by the innermost consciousness. Sincerity requires the lifting of all movements of mind, body, and action to the level of the highest consciousness, where there is no individuality, duality, or body consciousness. Sincerity is the unification and harmonization of man around that one central will, the divinity through which we speak, hear, think, and feel.

The Atman is revealed to that fortunate aspirant who surrenders himself without reserve to the Divine alone. For him, calmness, wisdom, and the sea of *ananda*, or inner bliss, overflow continuously. Merely wishing for self-surrender will not help. Merely assuming a mental attitude or having a number of inner experiences are not indications of self-surrender. Complete self-surrender requires a radical and total change in one's life. In this transformation all our habits and actions should be exposed to the divine light, for without complete self-surrender divine wisdom is not possible. For example, consider the life of an unenlightened man. He lives in the world much like an animal, expressing only his own mind, action, and speech, satisfying only his own wants and desires. An enlightened man, on the other hand, establishes himself in divinity and then brings forward that divinity from the innermost place inside himself, expressing it through mind, action, and speech. This is a sacred process, but it does not require any effort other than self-surrender.

Without complete self-surrender it is quite impossible for the aspirant to get anywhere near his goal, so in the course of this process he has to keep himself open to the call of the divine force, and allow that force to work through both his feelings and actions. If an aspirant does not surrender fully, he is still not allowing this force to work through him, but is imposing conditions upon it. Divine grace and bliss are ever present, but we remain sleeping, unprepared to receive it in our daily life. This is the root cause of our bondage and misery.

In the early stages of practicing self-surrender, sincere effort is indispensable, for surrender is not a thing which can be done in a fit of emotion or in a day. The human ego resists surrender. The mind has its own ideas and clings to them. The ego holds sway over the unenlightened person, who lives in a world ruled by ego. Unless someone sincerely desires to go beyond the mire of ego, self-surrender is impossible. For instance, if there is any surrender at all in the early stages of practice, it is usually of a dubious nature, with selfish demands hidden within it. But when spiritual powers awaken, true surrender occurs. A few aspirants do begin with a sincere and dynamic will to surrender, it is true. They constantly dwell in the Self, and having once accepted self-surrender, they will not question it. By so doing, they no longer obstruct their own path.

Surrender is the way of accepting the Divine. Surrender means to offer all one has and not insist on the primacy of one's own ideas and desires. Surrender empties the aspirant of ego and then fills him with divine truth. If he lets his mind take over, however, debating and deciding what is to be done, he will be in danger of losing touch with the divine force. Then the lower energies will begin to act for themselves, and this will lead to confusion. A simple offering of the self to the Divine, however, devoid of egoistic motives, brings immediate results. What is more, during this process the aspirant does not renounce the world and abandon his duties. He lives in the world. But he lives like the lotus which, though rooted in mud and supported by water, blossoms in air and sunlight.

· CHAPTER EIGHT ·

Samadhi

CONCENTRATION LEADS to one-pointedness, prolonged concentration leads to meditation, and meditation expands the mind into the superconscious state called samadhi in Patanjali's school of raja yoga. Patanjali, however, warns us that the practice of concentration must be accompanied by nonattachment, for one who tries to concentrate while remaining attached to the things of the world will either fail altogether, or his acquired power of concentration may lead him into great danger because he will use it for selfish ends.

The danger of attachment is exemplified in the technological progress of modern man. Through the study of the objective world he has been able to harness the forces of nature, but his attachment to the world has led him to misuse these forces. Atomic energy could be beneficial to all mankind, provided man develops an attitude of concern for humanity. Instead, it has become a threat to mankind's survival because man lacks an attitude of sympathy toward his fellowmen. The threat of nuclear catastrophe lies not in the nature of the atom, but rather in man's attachments.

Nonattachment does not signify renunciation of the world, although many people mistakenly interpret it in this way. It means perfecting the art of living here and now, performing duties skillfully, enjoying life and yet remaining free from dependency on, and addiction to, the objects of the world. When this technique is perfected, it is possible to live in the world and yet be free. The aspirant can use the forces of nature and the objects of the world as tools to further the expansion of consciousness. It is not necessary for anyone to renounce the world in order to attain samadhi.

How does one cultivate the attitude of nonattachment? An aspirant can start on the practical level of action. He can read about the great sages of any religion, study their lives, and model his life on theirs. This will lead to nonattachment in that his love for these ideals will begin to develop into love for all humanity. Another method of cultivating nonattachment is to discover *Brahman,* the central or absolute reality, manifested in the great sages of history. Realizing that these great men and women are individual projections of Brahman will soon lead to the realization that Brahman is not only in them but in each of us, and that we are all one.

There are two stages of samadhi. In *savikalpa* samadhi, the lower stage, the aspirant retains a sense of individuality. The seeker of truth sees the truth, but retains the sense of "I" as being different from the truth he experiences. He has to go beyond savikalpa samadhi to the stage of *nirvikalpa* samadhi, in which the seeker becomes one with the One. Here is to be found the union of *Atman* with Brahman. This stage transcends the stage of intense love and longing for the ideal, for now the seeker merges into his ideal, and no sense of duality remains.

Only one who is well-established in the stage of nirvikalpa

samadhi is an illumined yogi, and only he can truly guide other aspirants. Such a yogi is beyond the bondage of space, time, and causation, and is ever free, for it is possible for him to remain dissolved in Brahman and yet return to normal consciousness. He has achieved eternal bliss, which is undisturbed by any external conditions.

There may seem to be some resemblance between withdrawal from the external world in deep sleep and the highest state of nirvikalpa samadhi, but there is also a vast difference. One is an unconscious state while the other is the height of consciousness. Suppose two people go to see a king. One falls asleep before the king, while the other remains awake and enjoys the king's presence. The one who remains awake is like one in the blissful state of samadhi, while the other, being asleep, remains in the darkness of ignorance. In deep sleep, a person is very near to reality, but is not aware of reality.

Even during sleep a yogi remains fully awake to Brahman, and in the waking state he remains as if asleep to worldly attachments. In this divine union of lover and beloved, subject and object are dissolved in an ocean of supreme love. It is difficult to express the joy of this superconscious state. Personal experience is the only way to realize that eternal joy.

The word *samahitam*, which means "the state where all one's questions are answered," conveys the experiential quality of the state of samadhi. When all questions are answered and there is no doubt of any sort, then the mind soars beyond the level of the language in which it is accustomed to think. Samadhi does not occur at the level of thought or even feeling. This is why it is also called *bhavatita*, which means "beyond feelings." The state of samadhi, according to Patanjali's system, is considered to be the highest state attainable by yogis.

In other schools the word *samadhi* is not used. The meditative school of Buddhism, for instance, uses the word *nirvana* to describe the highest state of consciousness— through negation one experiences a void which is called nirvana. The philosophy of Advaita Vedanta describes something beyond nirvana, however. According to this school, the highest state is called *sakshatkara,* comparable to the state called samadhi in Patanjali's system. Here, according to raja yoga, when the individual consciousness expands itself to become universal consciousness, when *jiva* becomes *purusha,* then the word *samadhi* is used. It is a state beyond mind, action, and speech. It is the eighth and final rung on the yoga ladder and is achieved when the aspirant establishes his practice firmly, is able to continue his meditation for a long time without interruption yet with full devotion and reverence, and when the subtle sense of self-identity vanishes, allowing control of the latent modifications of the mind. Then samadhi is attained.

These practical hints will help you in your practice of meditation.

- Whatever spiritual method you follow, practice it systematically and regularly. The reward is immense.
- Laziness or sloth is the greatest enemy. Life is short, time is fleeting, and obstacles are many. Conquer them by sincere effort and prayer. Help comes from a higher level to sincere aspirants.
- Just as you eat morning, noon, afternoon, and night, so also will you have to meditate four times a day if you want to realize truth quickly. When you meditate, you will develop divine virtues, and a spiritual path is constructed in the mind. If you do not practice

regularly and become lax, the spiritual path will be washed away by a flood of impure thoughts. Regularity in meditation is of paramount importance.

- Meditation leads to the gate of intuitive knowledge, which is real knowledge. It is a mysterious ladder that takes the aspirant from earth to heaven. Truth is the Atman, but it is not possible to realize that truth without meditation. The paths are many, but you should follow only one path and practice only one method. All the different paths meet at the gate of the kingdom of Atman. Do not condemn anyone else's method or religion, but instead follow your own. Methods should not be changed again and again. The fundamentals of all great religions are the same.

The mind assumes the form of the objects it cognizes. When the aspirant continuously meditates on the inner Atman, he reaches the state of samadhi, and in this blissful state nothing is seen or heard. There is no body consciousness. There is only one consciousness, and that is the consciousness of the all-pervading Atman. This superconscious experience is called *turiya*, the "fourth state." The first three stages—waking, dreaming, and dreamless sleep—are common to everyone, and the fourth is latent in everyone. When a yogi establishes himself in the fourth state he experiences the living reality in his mind, action, and speech. Then he realizes, at all times and under all circumstances, that he is identical with *sat, chit,* and *ananda,* existence, knowledge, and bliss. Real spiritual life begins after the aspirant enters this state of superconsciousness. It is the state of divine peace.

Samadhi is not a state that can be attained easily, but if
it is achieved, supramental or intuitional knowledge is experienced. A person who does not possess this knowledge cannot
understand the true meaning of religion. In this state the
senses, mind, and intellect cease functioning; just as a river
merges into the ocean, so does the individual soul merge
into the supreme soul—and all limitations disappear.

So often beginners are afraid of this union because they
think their individuality might dissolve or be engulfed.
Actually, what occurs is not a loss of individuality, but an expansion of individuality. As long as the mind functions
within the limited realms of individual consciousness an aspirant can meditate, but never attain samadhi. The deepest
state of meditation, however, expands individual consciousness, and when it has expanded to its fullest capacity, that is
called samadhi—sleepless sleep, soundless sound, the highest
state of peace, or silence. However we may describe it, this
is the highest state a raja yogi can attain while at the same
time remaining aware of his attainment.

Many errors and failures face the aspirant on this divine
journey. One of the greatest of these is laziness. For instance, after a short period of meditation an aspirant may
feel like sleeping, and further meditation then becomes difficult. This is because he has not yet formed the habit of sitting in a steady posture and meditating on a single object.

During meditation the aspirant may feel that he is rising
from his seat. Some may feel that they are flying in the air.
Various people have different experiences, all of which are
functions of the mind, and all of which can become obstructions in the path of meditation. To the wise, they give
encouragement for further progress. Some hear melodious
sounds and others see light. Some receive spiritual joy, others

get both light and joy. These are temporary phases and may inspire those who pass through them. On the other hand, there will be those who will not see or experience any such visions. It is of no consequence. All these experiences are hallucinations, delusions, and illusory visions. They are not necessary for progress in meditation.

In the beginning the aspirant should avoid the artificial light of this world and try to make his abode in darkness so that he may see the living light within. Often visions arise from the inner world, but they come and go without leaving any permanent impressions on the mind. These are hallucinations based on objects previously seen, heard, or imagined. On the other hand, the more an aspirant meditates, the more his intuition is developed. It is this intuition which becomes the real guide.

The state of samadhi is not often experienced, but there are various paths described in the Upanishads to attain it: the path of negation, the path of selfless action, and the path of devotion. Emotional ecstasy, however, is not samadhi. Inspiration does help, but uncontrolled emotion is dangerous. In other words, inspiration from the guru is definitely beneficial, but ecstasy which is full of emotion cannot be called deep meditation.

A simile will give you an idea of samadhi. Four aspirants are at the foot of a mountain. They begin their search along different paths, using different methods. They describe the experiences of their journey differently—until they reach the top of the mountain. When they reach the summit, they all have the same view. There they agree that they are all at the same place. This experience cannot be shared with aspirants who have not completed the climb. Mere words of explanation are like the husk of a grain: one does not benefit from the nourishing properties of the grain's kernel by studying its husk.

The expression "All roads lead to Rome" is true, but when it comes to methods leading to self-realization, only raja yoga and its methods of training are scientific and subject to empirical verification. Raja yoga leads the student to the final state of realization, not by training the intellect alone, but by training the whole person, thus making him more useful to himself and to humanity.

Blessed are those who have attained samadhi.

Blessed are those who are striving to attain it.

Glossary

Adi Shankara   Literally "the first Shankara." Also known as Shankaracharya, Adi Shankara was the preeminent exponent of the nondual *(advaita)* school of Vedanta philosophy. In his thirty-two years of life (A.D. 788-820), he walked the length and breadth of India, organizing the monastic orders of swamis and, through his skill as a debater, reestablishing traditional Hinduism and its formal philosophy at a time when Buddhism was extremely popular. His commentary on the *Brahma Sutras* is considered a basic text on nondual philosophy, and he has also written commentaries on the major Upanishads and the Bhagavad Gita, as well as scores of devotional hymns. To this day the heads of the monasteries he established in the north, south, east, and west of the Indian subcontinent are considered authoritative centers in matters of philosophy and religion, and bear his name.

Advaita   "Nondual." The word refers to that school of Vedanta philosophy which stresses the absolute identity of the individual self *(Atman)* with the attributeless, nondual cosmic reality *(Brahman)* and the nonreality of the world as it is ordinarily experienced. It is described in Shankaracharya's commentaries on the *Brahma Sutras* and the major Upanishads.

Agni   "Fire." Agni is a Vedic deity who is the messenger of the gods, receiving offerings and transmuting them so they are suitable for consumption by the gods. In this way agni is a symbol for the vital energy within all things which transmutes and transforms them from within.

Ahankara   "I-maker" or ego. The function of the mind through which pure spirit *(purusha)* falsely identifies with the material and mental creation according to the Sankhya and Yoga philosophies.

Ahimsa The first of five moral restraints called yamas, which form the first step of the eightfold *(ashtanga)* system called raja yoga. Their purpose is to curtail behavior which is not conducive to spiritual growth. *Ahimsa* means "nonkilling; non-harming," and denotes nonviolence in thought, word, and deed. It leads to cultivation of all-encompassing love toward all of creation.

Ajna chakra "Command center." It is a center of consciousness corresponding to the nasociliary plexus of the physical nervous system, located between the eyebrows. It is called the command center because it is the seat of the mind in the waking state, and because when it is developed, all the centers below it come under its command. It governs the energy principle of the mind. Its power is awakened by the seed syllable Om. When the kundalini force rises through the *sushumna* channel to this center, *samadhi* with seed *(sabija* or *savikalpa)* is realized. (See also *chakra, kundalini, savikalpa, samadhi,* and *sushumna.)*

Akasha The Sanskrit word for the dynamic energy inherent in space itself. It is often translated as sky or ether, as well as the inner space, and the cave of the heart.

Anahata chakra "Unstruck center." This center of consciousness corresponds to the physical cardiac plexus located in the hollow just beneath the breastbone in the middle of the chest. It governs the energy principle inherent in air, symbolized by offerings of incense, and controls the cognitive sense of touch and the active sense of the genitals. Two interpenetrating triangles, like the Star of David, one inside the other, form the diagram of this chakra. Its color is said to be smoky gray or green. Its energies are awakened by the seed syllable *yam.* The chosen deity of one's mantra or the guru is meditated upon at this center, which is the center of feeling and emotion. It is a center for concentration on subtle sound vibrations *(nada),* and it is said that the *Atman* itself resides thumb-sized here in "the cave of the heart."

Ananda   Perfect joy. One of the three definitions of *Brahman: sat,* pure being, *chit,* pure consciousness, and *ananda,* pure joy.

Antahkarana   The "inner instrument" of the mind, consisting of *manas,* the active mind; *buddhi,* the rational and intuitive intelligence; *chitta,* the mind-stuff and reservoir of subtle impressions *(samskaras);* and *ahankara,* the instrument of identification, the ego or "I-maker."

Anu   The smallest, indivisible particle of matter. An atom.

Apah   Water. The energy principle of fluidity.

Apana   One of the five functions of the vital energy *(prana).* It governs elimination through the exhalation, kidneys, bladder, colon, rectum, and genitals.

Aparigraha   "Nonpossessiveness." The fifth of the series of moral restraints called *yamas* in yoga philosophy. Aparigraha cultivates the slackening of attachment to our own possessions so that things at our disposal become tools and not burdens. It is also intended to develop generosity toward those in need.

Ardha matsyendrasana   "Half-lord of fish posture." This is one in a series of hatha yoga postures which twist the spine laterally.

Asana   "Sitting; position; posture." The fourth of the eight limbs of raja yoga which emphasizes attainment of a steady and comfortable posture. It later evolved into the science of physical culture called hatha yoga, in which the word means any one of the hatha postures.

Ashtanga yoga   "Eight-limbed yoga" refers to the eight steps of classical raja yoga as they are explained in Patanjali's *Yoga Sutra.* The eight limbs are *yama,* moral restraints, *niyama,* moral practices, *asana,* posture, *pranayama,* control of the breath and prana, *pratyahara,* withdrawal and control of the senses, *dharana,* concentration, *dhyana,* meditation, and finally *samadhi,* superconscious meditation.

Ashta-prakriti The eight principles or elements of the material and mental universe in Sankhya philosophy. They are solidity (earth), liquidity (water), heat (fire), gaseousness (air), space, *manas* (lower mind), *buddhi* (rational and intuitive intelligence), and *ahankara* (ego).

Asteya "Nonstealing." Asteya is the third of the *yamas.* It includes nonmisappropriation of money and nonacceptance of unethical gifts, as well as nonstealing, in order to purge the student of desire for others' possessions.

Asu The pranas or vital energies.

Atman The individual self which, according to Vedanta philosophy is identical to the cosmic Self, the absolute reality, *Brahman.* It is similar to the *purusha,* or pure spirit, of Sankhya and Yoga. That pure spirit is said to be shrouded by five sheaths: the physical body, the body of vital energy *(prana),* the active mental body, the body of knowledge, and the body of perfect joy *(ananda).* In meditative practice a yogi gradually pierces these sheaths until he reaches his inner self, Atman, in the highest stage of samadhi.

Atma-shakti The power and potential of the Self. (See also *shakti.)*

Avidya Ignorance of the real nature of oneself and the world.

Bandha "Bondage." The absence of spiritual freedom as a result of *avidya* (ignorance). The opposite of spiritual liberation which is the goal of yoga. Also, "lock." Certain bodily gestures or contractions which establish connections between energy channels *(nadis)* and aid in controlling the flow of vital energy *(prana)* in the practice of pranayama.

Bhakti yoga The spiritual path in which a devotional relationship is cultivated with a chosen deity. In bhakti yoga the energies which are usually dissipated in random emotions are focused on one's beloved deity, and so become a force propelling the student in a definite spiritual direction.

Bhastrika   "Bellows." A breathing exercise in which the abdominal muscles and diaphragm function like a bellows, with forced inhalation and exhalation of equal length.

Bhava   "Mood." A state of strong emotion. The word is also used to describe higher states of emotional ecstasy in the path of devotion, bhakti yoga.

Bhujangasana   The cobra posture.

Bija   "Seed." A bija mantra is a meaningless sound originally perceived by a sage, with enormous latent energy which grows into a tree of knowledge if this seed is nourished by constant repetition of the mantra.

Bindu   A point marking the limit of the conscious mind's capacity, which is pierced in higher states of meditation in order to bring an aspirant to the superconscious state of samadhi. This technique is called "bursting the bindu," or *bindu bhedana* in Sanskrit.

Brahma   The first member of the Hindu trinity, characterizing the principle of *rajas*, or energy. He is therefore the lord of creation and *prajapati*, the lord of all creatures.

Brahmacharya   "Walking in Brahman." The fourth of the yamas, or moral restraints. Brahmacharya is also described as controlling one's energies and curbing their wastage through sensory dissipation by using the senses carefully and skillfully. Since the greatest loss of energy occurs in the act of sex, this term is often used to mean sexual celibacy specifically. It is more properly celibacy of all the senses, cognitive and active.

Brahman   The absolute reality of the universe, the cosmic Self which is described in Vedanta philosophy as *sat*, pure being, truth, and reality; *chit,* pure consciousness; and *ananda,* pure joy. It exists, however, beyond all qualities and attributes, so the Upanishads teach that the definition most free of error is *neti, neti,* "neither this nor that."

Brahma-randhra   "Hole or gate of *Brahman."* A spiritual center of consciousness near the fontanel through which a yogi leaves his body voluntarily when the usefulness of his physical body is exhausted.

Buddhi   The faculty of discrimination; the intuitive and intellectual intelligence.

Chakra   "Wheel." Cognate to Latin *circus,* English *circle.* The chakras are centers of consciousness in the subtle body corresponding to the major nerve plexuses of the gross physical nervous system situated along the spinal cord. Each center controls a certain energy principle. There are seven major centers corresponding to the principles of solidity (earth), liquidity (water), heat (fire), gaseousness (air), space, mind, and the pure consciousness of the Self. These energy principles, in turn, correspond to particular sensations of subtle (nonphysical) light and sound, certain geometric patterns called *yantras,* which are used to depict the centers as well as for meditational exercises, and certain *bijas* (seed syllables) or sound vibrations which form the basis for the science of mantra. The repetition of these seed syllables helps to awaken the energy in a particular center.

Chakrasana   The wheel posture.

Chitta   The pool of subconscious mind-stuff into which all the impressions gathered by the senses are thrown, as it were, and from the bottom of which they rise to create a constant stream of random thoughts and associations. According to Patanjali, the codifier of yoga philosophy, "Yoga is the cessation of changes and modifications of chitta." *(Yoga Sutra* 1.2).

Dhanurasana   The bow posture.

Dharana   Concentration. The process of bringing the mind, the natural tendency of which is to jump from object to object, to voluntary, relaxed attention on a single object. It is the sixth of the eight limbs of yoga described in the *Yoga Sutra*.

Dhyana   "Meditation." When the mind has become withdrawn from the senses and concentrated, it achieves a steady, natural flow of attention toward one object.

Divya-chaksu   "Divine eye." The "third eye" which corresponds to the clairvoyant faculty of the fully awakened *ajna* chakra between the two eyebrows.

Divya-drishti   "Divine sight."

Dosha   Wind, bile, and phlegm are the three doshas, or bodily constituents, the imbalance of which leads to disease according to Ayurveda, the indigenous Indian medical system.

Guna   "Attribute; quality." The three gunas of *prakriti*, or matter, are *sattva* (equilibrium), *rajas* (dynamism), and *tamas* (inertia).

Guru   According to the oral tradition of yoga, the syllable *gu* signifies darkness, and the syllable *ru* signifies a dispeller, so the guru or spiritual guide is the dispeller of the darkness of ignorance. He is one who has tested all methods of yoga and experienced everything to be experienced on the spiritual path so that he may guide students past illusory experiences, teaching them to utilize properly the energies which they are attempting to rechannel. The purpose of the guru, as an external person, is to lead the student to the inner teacher, one's own true Self.

Halasana   The plow posture.

Hatha yoga   The science of physical culture which developed out of the third limb of raja yoga, *asana*. It attempts, through postures and cleansing exercises, to prepare the student for higher practices in yoga. It also denotes the first four limbs of raja yoga—*yama, niyama, asana,* and *pranayama,* which are known as the external limbs.

Hiranyagarbha "Golden womb; golden egg." The cosmic mind, regarded as the first and true teacher of yoga.

Ida One of the three principle energy channels flowing in the spinal cord. It controls the breath in the left nostril. It is said to be feminine and lunar in nature, inclining the mind toward intuition, creativity, passivity, calmness, and sleep. In the word *hatha* it is symbolized by the syllable *tha.* The goal of hatha yoga is to join the two channels, *pingala* and *ida, ha* and *tha,* into the central channel, *sushumna,* where the mind becomes inclined toward stillness, joy, and meditation.

Ishvara-pranidhana The fifth of the five moral practices in the yoga system. It means "surrender to the Lord," both in a devotional sense and in the sense of surrender to your own true Self. It must become, in practice, learning to see your Self in others and cultivating surrender of ego to that Self.

Japa Mental repetition of a mantra, which gradually awakens the energy vibrations of which the syllables are the gross representation.

Jnana yoga "Discipline of knowledge." Jnana yoga involves cultivation of one's intelligence, starting from the rational intellect and developing toward intuition. Its goal is *chit,* pure consciousness.

Kaivalya "Isolation" of *purusha,* or pure spirit, from his false identification with *prakriti,* or material nature. It is the final goal of spiritual practice in the Sankhya and Yoga philosophies, and is the subject of the last chapter of the *Yoga Sutra: "Kaivalya Pada."*

Kantha A part of the subtle body corresponding to the area of the physical larynx.

Kapalabhati   "Shining of the skull; glowing forehead." A breathing technique in which the abdominal muscles and diaphragm make a fast and forceful exhalation followed by a passive inhalation.

Karma yoga   "Discipline of action" in which selfless activity without desire for personal gain is cultivated. In this way one gradually cuts back on the amount of new impressions (the seeds of future action and of rebirth) gathered by the subconscious. One's actions are gradually purified as meditation is slowly brought into active life.

Karya-brahman   The cosmic mind. (See also *hiranyagarbha.*)

Kumbhaka   The method of retaining the breath in more advanced exercises of pranayama. Retention should not be practiced without the guidance of an experienced and qualified teacher.

Kundalini   "Coiled one." The concentrated, fundamental life-energy of an individual. In its latent state it is symbolized by a coiled serpent sleeping in the lowest center of consciousness (*muladhara* chakra) at the base of the spine. The goal of preliminary yoga practice is to awaken this energy and channel it upward through the *sushumna* to the highest center, the thousand-petaled lotus. As the energy pierces each center on its journey upward, it blooms, as it were, and gradually one's whole being is transformed and perfected.

Kundalini yoga   A system of practices which includes the use of mantras, *yantras* (the diagrammatical counterpart of mantra practice), *mudras* (particular postures and gestures), and breathing exercises to awaken and raise the latent kundalini force.

Laya yoga   "Yoga of absorption." A system of meditational practices in which the awareness of grosser elements is progressively absorbed into finer ones.

Mahat   In Sankhya philosophy this is the first entity to manifest from primordial nature, *prakriti*. It is the cosmic counterpart of the individual *buddhi*.

Manas   "Active mind." This word is also used loosely as a synonym for the *antahkarana*.

Manaspati   "Lord of the mind *(manas)*." That which controls the mind.

Manipura chakra   "Jeweled city." The center of consciousness which corresponds to the solar plexus located in the navel area. This center governs the energy principle of heat and is symbolized by fire. It controls the cognitive sense of sight and the active sense of elimination through the bowels. Its power is awakened by the seed syllable *ram*. The diagram of the manipura chakra is an upward triangle, and it is represented by the color red.

Mantra   A combination of syllables or words corresponding to a particular energy vibration. The student, when initiated by a qualified teacher, utilizes the mantra as an object for meditation, and as he practices over a period of time, it gradually leads his meditation deeper and deeper. It is the condensed essence of all the teaching the guru has to give. Through his constant practice of repeating the mantra both within meditation and in active life, the power of the mantra and its essential teaching will gradually unfold as its latent mental and spiritual energies are released.

Mantra yoga   The set of practices in which particular revealed phrases, words, and syllables (and in higher states of meditation, vibrations of subtle sound) are utilized as objects of meditation to awaken a student's spiritual potential. The essential technique is *japa*, or mental repetition.

Matsyasana   The fish posture.

Mayurasana   The peacock posture.

Merudanda   "Axis of Mount Meru; the Meru pole." The mythical mountain Meru is considered the axis of the earth. The merudanda is the inner axis corresponding to the physical spinal column along which rises the subtle *sushumna* channel. The kundalini force rises along this axis to the highest center as consciousness "going up the mountain," as it were.

Muladhara chakra   "Foundation; root-support center." It corresponds to the sacral or pelvic nerve plexus at the base of the physical spine. It is the resting place of the unactivated, fundamental life-energy, kundalini, symbolized by a coiled, sleeping serpent. Yoga practices attempt to awaken that energy and raise and purify it gradually until it reaches the highest center of consciousness where self-realization is attained. This center governs the energy principle, earth (solidity), the cognitive sense of smell, and the active sense of mobility. It is represented diagrammatically as a square, its color is yellow, and its power is awakened by the seed syllable *lam.* In ritual offerings one would offer fruits or fragrances as symbols of this principle.

Nadi   A channel in the subtle body for the nonphysical vital force called prana which runs roughly parallel to the physical nervous system. Yoga texts claim that there are between 72,000 and 350,000 such subtle channels. The three primary ones are *ida, pingala,* and *sushumna,* which run along the spinal column and control the flow of breath in the left nostril, the right nostril, and both nostrils together, respectively.

Nadi shodhanam   "Purifying the *nadis.*" A breathing exercise that purifies the nadis in preparation for the higher practice of pranayama. Also known as channel purification or alternate nostril breathing, it attempts to quiet the mind and regulate the breath by establishing a slow, even rhythm, without a pause between inhalation and exhalation.

Nididhyasana   Another Sanskrit term for *dhyana*, or meditation. Contemplation in jnana yoga. It is one of the four steps in the intellectual process.

Nirvikalpa samadhi   "Samadhi without distinctions" or the *nirbija*, "seedless," samadhi. The highest stage of samadhi in which there is no "seed" or object of meditation. There are no distinctions between the knower and the known; there is only knowing *(chit)*, the pure consciousness aspect of *Brahman*.

Niyama   "Observances; practices." The second limb of the eight-limbed system of raja yoga described in the *Yoga Sutra* of Patanjali. While the five *yamas*, or moral restraints, gradually curtail behaviors which create obstacles to growth, the *niyamas*, also five in number, attempt to cultivate positive habits which are conducive to self-realization. The niyama practices are purity of the body and mind *(shaucha)*, contentment *(santosha)*, practices to perfect the functioning of body, mind and senses *(tapas)*, self-study *(svadhyaya)*, and surrender of the ego to the higher Self *(Ishvara-pranidhana)*. For a more detailed explanation, each niyama has been listed separately.

Om   The highest of mantras. The sum total of the celestial and cosmic sound principles, it is said to be the mother of all speech. (Say anything with your lips closed and all that comes out is *Om.*) Its three letters, a, u and m (which in Sanskrit phonetics combine into *Om)*, represent the elements of all trinities as well as the three qualities *(gunas)* of the material and mental creation *(prakriti)*. There is also a silent fourth syllable symbolizing the transcendent fourth state of pure spirit, *turiya* or *samadhi*. A symbol of the highest realization and knowledge, Om precedes and follows all prayers and recitations of texts in Indian tradition, and is found in many mantras. From Vedic times it has also been known as *pranava*.

Pada   "Foot; part; chapter." This word is used in the names of the four chapters of Patanjali's *Yoga Sutra:* "*Samadhi Pada*," the chapter on samadhi; "*Sadhana Pada*," the chapter concerning methods of practice; *"Vibhuti Pada,"* the chapter on attainments; and *"Kaivalya Pada,"* the chapter on isolation (of pure spirit from material nature).

Padmasana   The lotus posture.

Paramatman   The supreme Self which is one with the individual Self *(jivatman)* in Vedanta philosophy.

Paricchinna   "Cut off; limited." It refers to the mind in its ordinary, limited functioning.

Paschimottanasana   The posterior stretch posture.

Pingala   The *nadi,* or energy channel, which is one of the three running parallel to the spinal column. It controls the flow of breath in the right nostril. When this channel becomes active one's behavior is characterized by rationality, activity, and energy. One might also feel an increase in body heat. The effect of this flow of *prana* is said to be solar and masculine; it is the opposite of the left flow, *ida,* which is said to be feminine and lunar.

Prakriti   "That which makes forth." In Sankhya and Yoga philosophy it is the material and mental creation with which pure spirit *(purusha)* has falsely identified itself on account of ego, the "I-maker" *(ahankara).* The goal of yoga is the isolation *(kaivalya)* of purusha from prakriti—the identification of pure spirit with itself. Prakriti is said to have three attributes *(gunas),* or tendencies: balance or purity *(sattva),* energy *(rajas),* and inertia *(tamas).* Everything in the material universe is said to be some combination of these three tendencies.

Prana   The vital force or life energy in any living being which exists in a subtle, nonphysical form. It flows through a system of energy channels *(nadis)* which make up the subtle body. The different ways in which particular flows of energy affect the body have been given special names such as *prana, apana, samana, udana,* and *vyana.* The flow called *prana* regulates inhalation; *apana*, excretion and exhalation; *samana*, digestion and distribution of nutrients and energy; *udana*, upward movement of *prana* in coughs, sneezes, peristalsis, and death; *vyana* pervades the whole skeletal, muscular, and nervous structure and controls blood flow, relaxation, and tension.

Pranayama   The science of gradually lengthening and controlling the physical breath in order to gain control over the movements of *prana* through the subtle body in higher stages of practice. It is the fourth of the eight steps of yoga described by Patanjali.

Pratyahara   The fifth of the eight limbs of yoga. Pratyahara is the withdrawal and control of the senses. It protects the mind from distractions during concentration, meditation, and samadhi.

Prithivi   Earth, the densest substance of creation.

Purusha   In Sankhya philosophy this is the pure spirit, the indwelling person in everything. It exists in proximity to material and mental creation *(prakriti)* on account of false identification of the ego. The ultimate aim of yoga practice is to discriminate between the two, to exist in pure spirit alone *(kaivalya)*.

Raja yoga   "Royal path." Raja yoga is the classical system of yoga philosophy and practice codified by the sage Patanjali in the *Yoga Sutra*. It is also known as the eight-limbed *(ashtanga)* yoga because it is divided into eight steps, some of which were elaborated into separate, specialized areas of discipline. Hatha yoga, for instance, is the science of psychophysical culture which developed out of the third limb, asana, or posture. Raja yoga is also used to signify the last four limbs taken together: *pratyahara*, or control of the senses; *dharana*, or concentration; *dhyana*, or meditation; and *samadhi*, or superconscious meditation.

Rajas   One of the three *gunas*, or qualities, of *prakriti*, material nature. It is the active, dynamic attribute of nature.

Rishi   A seer, especially one to whom a mantra is revealed.

Sadhana   "Accomplishing; fulfilling." Sadhana is the word for a student's sincere efforts along a particular path of practice toward self-realization. It is the subject of the second chapter of the *Yoga Sutra: "Sadhana Pada."*

Sahasrara   The highest center of consciousness called the "thousand-petaled lotus," which corresponds to the ventricular cavity of the physical brain. When the kundalini reaches this center, the unseeded *(nirbija)* samadhi without distinctions *(nirvikalpa)* is realized, and the *samskaras,* or seeds of future actions, are burned in the highest knowledge. At this point the aspirant becomes prepared for liberation.

Samadhi   The superconscious state which is the last of the eight limbs of yoga. In samadhi of the seeded variety *(sabija* or *savikalpa),* one's superconscious mind directly experiences the object of meditation—the *bija,* or seed—in its true nature. In seedless samadhi there is no longer a need for an object of meditation, and one gains the knowledge of one's own self and its identity to the cosmic Self *(Brahman).* There can be no distinction *(vikalpa)* between the knower and the known; there is only perfect knowing. Samadhi is the topic of the first chapter of Patanjali's *Yoga Sutra.*

Samana   One of the five flows of prana. It controls digestion and metabolism and is situated between the heart and the navel.

Sambhuti   Another term for the cosmic mind.

Samskara   Latent tendencies hidden in the unconscious.

Sankalpa   "Resolve." The determination to carry something through to completion.

Sankhya   A system of philosophy based on the duality of material nature *(prakriti)* and pure spirit *(purusha).* The goal of Sankhya is to discriminate between these two aspects of one's own being and attain the isolation of purusha, which is called *kaivalya* (existence in pure spirit). Sankhya forms the philosophical basis for the practice of yoga. It was systematized by the sage Kapila around 600 B.C. and is outlined in a number of texts such as the *Sankhya-Karika*.

Santosha   The second of the five niyamas, or moral practices, through which one cultivates evenmindedness and contentment regardless of one's material situation. It is not to be confused with apathy or laziness.

Sarvangasana   "Posture for all limbs." The shoulderstand.

Sat   "Pure being." One of the three aspects attributed to the nondual Brahman. (See also *ananda, Brahman,* and *chit).*

Sattva   Possessed of the quality of harmony, purity, and balance. It is one of the three qualities *(gunas)* of material nature, or *prakriti,* in the Sankhya philosophy.

Satya   The second of the five *yamas,* or moral restraints. It involves truthfulness to oneself and to others.

Savikalpa samadhi   The lower stages of samadhi in which the student becomes one with the inner nature of the object or seed *(bija)* of his meditation and experiences it directly. There are eight stages of savikalpa samadhi which are described in the first chapter of Patanjali's *Yoga Sutra: "Samadhi Pada."*

Setu bandhasana   The bridge posture.

Shakti   Derived from the Sanskrit root *shak* meaning "to be capable of." It means "power; energy; force." It usually denotes the active power of some deity or energy principle. For instance, kundalini is also called *chit-shakti,* the power of consciousness or the consciousness force.

Shalabhasana   The locust posture.

Shaucha   The first *niyama,* or moral practice, which cleans and purifies body, mind, and spirit so that all parts of the personality function properly.

Shavasana   The corpse relaxation posture.

Shirshasana   The headstand.

Shiva   One of the three aspects of divinity, corresponding to the three qualities of the manifest universe *(gunas)*. Shiva is the third, representing dissolution, or that through which all things return to their essential nature *(tamas)*. He also represents the consciousness principle, of which kundalini, or *chit-shakti,* is the active power. In the tantric system of yoga practice, the goal is to raise that vital energy to the highest center of consciousness, the thousand-petaled lotus, so that Shiva and his *Shakti* may become one, producing the highest state of consciousness.

Siddhasana   The accomplished posture. A sitting posture used for breathing exercises and meditation.

Siddhis   "Attainments; powers" which appear when one ascends the higher rungs of yoga practice. They are a dangerous temptation and can become obstacles on the path. They are also called *vibhutis* and are discussed in the third chapter of the *Yoga Sutra: "Vibhuti Pada."*

Sukhasana   The easy posture. A sitting posture used for breathing exercises and meditation.

Sushumna   The central channel, or *nadi,* for the subtle energy of consciousness *(chit)* and life *(jiva)*. One of three channels that flow (approximately) along the spinal column. The goal of preliminary breathing exercises is to open this central channel so that both nostrils are flowing equally, and then the mind enters a joyful state where it naturally tends to meditate.

Sutra   "Thread." A sutra is a brief aphorism of the kind used by Indian philosophers to record the progression of the main ideas (the thread of meaning) of a philosophical system. They are terse sentences from which all that is unnecessary has been eliminated. The sutras, especially those from the oral tradition, cannot be understood without commentaries.

Svadhishthana chakra   The center of consciousness called "her own abode," corresponding to the plexus located just above the genital area. The energy principle centered here is liquidity, symbolized ritualistically in offerings of water. It controls the cognitive sense of taste and the active sense of the hands. Its diagram is a crescent, colored milky-white, and its energies are awakened by the seed syllable *vam*.

Svadhyaya   The fourth of five *niyamas,* or moral practices. Through svadhyaya one cultivates self-study. It includes the study of scripture and spiritual subjects which lead the mind to meditative pursuits; the examinations of one's actions in life; and *japa,* the incessant repetition of one's mantra. It involves the experiential testing of truths accepted by the intellect. This assists in the growth of rational intellect toward intuition. (See also *jnana yoga).*

Svarodaya   The yogic science of breath.

Svastikasana   The auspicious posture. A sitting posture used for breathing exercises and meditation.

Talu   Area of the subtle body corresponding to the base of the physical skull.

Tamas   The quality of inertia. One of the three qualities *(gunas)* of material creation *(prakriti).*

Tapas   "Fire; heat." This is the third *niyama,* or moral observance, and includes austerities used to perfect the body, mind, and senses, and to give rise to fervent determination for realization.

Tattva   "That-ness." *Tattva* denotes the distinctive and elemental state of a thing. In Sankhya philosophy the tattvas are the evolutes of primal *prakriti,* especially the five physical states of matter (for example, the solidity of earth, the liquidity of water, the heat of fire, and so forth).

Tejas   The luminosity that emanates from the mind.

Trataka   The practice of gazing in order to strengthen concentration.

Turiya   "Fourth." The superconscious state of samadhi which transcends the three states of waking, dreaming, and deep sleep.

Udana   One of the five major flows of *prana.* It controls the region of the body above the larynx and governs our senses (sight, hearing, smell, and taste), coughing, sneezing, and peristalsis. It is also the prana instrumental in the process of death.

Upanishads   The most philosophical portion of the Vedas and the most recent in the series of Vedic texts. The essence of the Vedic teachings is condensed in these writings.

Ustrasana   The camel posture.

Vayu   The Sanskrit term for the energy principle of air, or gaseousness. The word is also sometimes used for the *pranas.*

Vedantin   Those who profess the Vedanta philosophy. The word usually refers to the followers of the nondual or Advaita Vedanta school who are also called *advaitins.*

Vibhu   "All-pervading." It is through the realization of the all-pervading nature of the Self that a yogi gains control over his environment and, consequently, over what appear to be miraculous powers, or *vibhutis.* (See also *siddhi).* The word also refers to a theory which holds that all minds are linked ultimately to a cosmic mind, *hiranyagarbha.*

Vishuddha chakra   "Purified center." This center corresponds to the base of the throat, along the spinal column. The principle of space is controlled from this chakra, which is represented by a circle and the color blue. It is symbolized ritualistically in offerings by the opening and closing of flowers. The cognitive sense of hearing and the active sense of the mouth are governed from this center whose power is awakened by the seed syllable *ham.*

Vrischikasana   The scorpion posture.

Vritti   "Wave; modification." The train of thoughts which moves through the mind is spoken of as being made up of *vrittis,* or waves, arising from the deep subconscious reservoir of *chitta,* the mind-stuff. Yoga is defined in the *Yoga Sutra* as the cessation of these chitta vrittis.

Vyana   One of the five primary flows of *prana.* Vyana pervades the whole skeletal, muscular, nervous, and circulatory apparatus of the body and regulates its tension and relaxation.

Yama   "Restraint." In yoga five moral restraints form the first of the eight steps of the royal path, raja yoga. The purpose of these abstentions is to gradually eliminate habits of emotional behavior which are not conducive to spiritual progress so that a student may be at peace with his conscience. The five are nonviolence of thought, word, and deed *(ahimsa);* truthfulness and nonlying *(satya);* nonstealing and not coveting others' possessions *(asteya);* nonpossessiveness and nonattachment to one's own possessions *(aparigraha);* celibacy of all the active and cognitive senses and the mind *(brahmacharya).* (For a more detailed description, each of the yamas has been listed separately.)

Yoga   The school of Indian philosophy, closely related to Sankhya, which, in addition to its philosophical tenets, includes a whole system of practices through which philosophical claims can be tested in actual experience as the student perfects himself physically, mentally, and spiritually. It is a universal, exact science of developing human potential and has evolved over perhaps five thousand years of experimentation by its practitioners. It was first codified by the sage Patanjali in his *Yoga Sutra* around the second century, B.C. The word *yoga* is generated from the Sanskrit root *yuj* which means "to join or apply." Yoga means "union" as well as the systematic application of certain practices with tested and proven effects and benefits. In this sense of application yoga also comes to mean discipline, as in jnana yoga, the "discipline of knowledge."

Yoga mudra   The symbol of yoga. A particular hatha yoga posture.

Yoga Sutra   A manual of 196 aphorisms devoted to the royal path, raja yoga, composed by the sage Patanjali circa 200 B.C. It forms the basic outline on which all systems of yoga philosophy and practice base their techniques.

Recommendations
for Further Study

The following will be especially helpful in advancing your understanding and practice of yoga and meditation:

The Art of Joyful Living . . . . Swami Rama

Inner Quest . . . . Pandit Rajmani Tigunait, Ph.D.

Living with the Himalayan Masters . . . . . Swami Rama

Meditation and Its Practice . . . . Swami Rama

Path of Fire and Light,
Volumes I and II . . . . Swami Rama

The Power of Mantra and the Mystery of
Initiation . . . . Pandit Rajmani Tigunait, Ph.D.

Science of Breath . . . . Swami Rama, Rudolph
Ballentine, M.D., and Alan Hymes, M.D.

Superconscious Meditation . . . Usharbudh Arya, D. Litt.

Transition to Vegetarianism . . . . . Rudolph Ballentine,
M.D.

Yoga: Mastering the Basics . . . . . . Sandra Anderson and
Rolf Sovik, Psy.D.

You may also find several relaxation and meditation tapes to be useful, including:

Guided Meditation for Beginners

Guided Yoga Relaxations

A Guide to Intermediate Meditation

First Step Toward Advanced Meditation

Learn to Meditate

31 and 61 Points

These and other books, tapes and DVDs on meditation are available from the Himalayan Institute Press. For a catalog or further information, call 800-822-4547 or 570-253-5551, e-mail: hibooks@HimalayanInstitute.org, or fax: 570-647-1552.

For students interested in practicing japa, a Japa Kit containing full instructions and a mala (yoga rosary) is also available.

Visit our website at www.HimalayanInstitute.org.

About the Author

ONE OF THE greatest adepts, teachers, writers, and humanitarians of the 20th century, Swami Rama is the founder of the Himalayan Institute®. Born in Northern India, he was raised from early childhood by a Himalayan sage, Bengali Baba. Under the guidance of his master he traveled from monastery to monastery and studied with a variety of Himalayan saints and sages, including his grandmaster, who was living in a remote region of Tibet. In addition to this intense spiritual training, Swami Rama received higher education in both India and Europe. From 1949 to 1952, he held the prestigious position of Shankaracharya of Karvirpitham in South India. Thereafter, he returned to his master to receive further training at his cave monastery, and finally in 1969, came to the United States where he founded the Himalayan Institute. His best known work, *Living with the Himalayan Masters,* reveals the many facets of this singular adept and demonstrates his embodiment of the living tradition of the East.

Main building of the international headquarters, Honesdale, Pa., USA

The Himalayan Institute

A LEADER IN THE FIELD OF YOGA, meditation, spirituality, and holistic health, the Himalayan Institute® was founded by Swami Rama of the Himalayas. The mission of the Himalayan Institute® is Swami Rama's mission to discover and embrace the sacred link, the spirit of human heritage that unites East and West, spirituality and science, and ancient wisdom and modern technology. Using time tested techniques of yoga, ayurveda, integrative medicine, principles of spirituality, and holistic health, the Institute has brought health, happiness, peace, and prosperity to the lives of tens of thousands for more than a quarter of a century. At the Himalayan Institute® you will learn techniques to develop a healthy body, a clear mind, and a joyful spirit, bringing a qualitative change within and without.

The Himalayan Institute's headquarters is located on a beautiful 400-acre campus in the rolling hills of the Pocono Mountains of northeastern Pennsylvania. In the spiritually vibrant atmosphere of the Institute, you will meet students and seekers from all walks of life who are participating in programs in hatha yoga, meditation, stress reduction, ayurveda, nutrition, spirituality, and Eastern philosophy. Choose from weekend or weeklong seminars, month long self-transformation programs, longer residential programs, spiritual retreats, and custom-designed holistic health services, pancha karma, and rejuvenation programs. In the peaceful setting of the Institute, you will relax and discover the best of yourself. We invite you to join us in the ongoing process of personal growth and development.

Swami Rama transplanted his Himalayan cave to the Poconos in the form of the Himalayan Institute®. The wisdom you will find at the Institute will direct you to the safe, secure, peaceful, and joyful cave in your own heart.

"Knowledge of various paths leads you to form your own conviction.
The more you know, the more you decide to learn"
–Swami Rama

PROGRAMS AND SERVICES INCLUDE:
- Weekend or extended seminars and workshops
- Meditation retreats and advanced meditation instruction
- Hatha yoga teachers' training
- Residential programs for self-development
- Holistic health services and pancha karma at the Institute's Center for Health and Healing

- Spiritual excursions
- Varcho Veda® herbal products
- Himalayan Institute Press
- *Yoga International* magazine
- Sanskrit correspondence course

To request a free copy of our quarterly guide to programs, or for further information, call 800-822-4547 or 570-253-5551, write to Himalayan Institute, 952 Bethany Turnpike, Building 1, Honesdale, PA, 18431, USA, or visit our website at www.HimalayanInstitute.org.

HIMALAYAN INSTITUTE®
PRESS

THE HIMALAYAN INSTITUTE PRESS has long been regarded as "The Resource for Holistic Living." We publish dozens of titles, as well as audio and video tapes, that offer practical methods for living harmoniously and achieving inner balance. Our approach addresses the whole person—body, mind, and spirit—integrating the latest scientific knowledge with ancient healing and self-development techniques.

As such, we offer a wide array of titles on physical and psychological health and well-being, spiritual growth through meditation and other yogic practices, as well as translations of yogic scriptures.

Our yoga accessories include the Japa Kit for meditation practice and the Neti Pot™, the ideal tool for sinus and allergy sufferers. The Varcho Veda® line of quality herbal extracts is now available to enhance balanced health and well-being.

Subscriptions are available to a bimonthly magazine, *Yoga International*, which offers thought-provoking articles on all aspects of meditation and yoga, including yoga's sister science, ayurveda.

For a free catalog call 800-822-4547 or 570-253-5551, email hibooks@HimalayanInstitute.org, fax 570-647-1552, write to the Himalayan Institute Press, 630 Main Street, Suite 350, Honesdale, PA, 18431, USA, or visit our website at www.HimalayanInstitute.org.